Ho Chi Minh
호치민

Biography Comic
who? **27** Ho Chi Minh

초판 1쇄 인쇄 2011년 4월 8일
초판 2쇄 발행 2013년 7월 5일

지은이 이숙자
그린이 스튜디오 청비
번역 로라 김
감수 김수희
펴낸이 김선식

Chief Story Creator 김정미
Story Creator 채정은
Design Creator 김경민
Marketing Creator 신문수

4th Creative Story Team 김선영, 이유미, 김선민, 전해인, 최수아
Creative Design Dept. 박효영
Creative Management Team 김성자, 송현주, 권송이, 김민아, 윤이경, 한선미
Creative Marketing Dept. 최창규, 이주화, 이상혁, 박현미, 백미숙
  Communication Team 서선행
  Contents Rights Team 김미영

펴낸곳 (주)다산북스
주소 서울시 마포구 서교동 395-27번지
전화 02-702-1724(기획편집) 02-703-1725(마케팅) 02-704-1724(경영지원)
팩스 02-703-2219
이메일 dasanbooks@hanmail.net
홈페이지 www.dasanbooks.com
출판등록 2005년 12월 23일 제313-2005-00277호

필름 출력 스크린그래픽센타 **종이** 월드페이퍼(주) **인쇄 · 제본** (주)현문

ISBN 978-89-6370-455-5 14740
SET 978-89-6370-438-8

* 책값은 표지 뒤쪽에 있습니다.
* 파본은 구입하신 서점에서 교환해드립니다.
* 이 책은 저작권법에 의하여 보호를 받는 저작물이므로 무단 전재와 복제를 금합니다.

who?
Ho Chi Minh
호치민

글 **이숙자** | 그림 **스튜디오 청비** | 번역 **로라 김** | 감수 **김수희**

Dasan Kid

Ho Chi Minh

Vietnamese politician, May 19, 1890 ~ September 2, 1969

A leader who loved his people, Ho Chi Minh, was born in 1890 in a small farming village in Vietnam called Kim Lien. At the time of his birth, Vietnam was colonized by France.

While he was a student, he saw Vietnamese people getting persecuted and participated in a demonstration to help the farmers, resulting in his expulsion from school. After this incident, Minh grappled with what he could do to aid his country and decided to travel to various countries to learn more about the vast world. He got a job as an assistant to the chef on a French ship and traveled all over the world and spoke of what was happening in Vietnam.

As a result of his actions, he became a wanted man by the French police and was not allowed to return to his motherland for thirty years. Although he was physically restrained, Minh did not stop working for Vietnam's independence.

After completing the preparations, Minh returned to Vietnam at the age of 51 with communist ideology and initiated the Vietnam independence movement (Viet Minh). He led the independence movement against France, Japan, and other powerful nations in intense battles. In the end, Vietnam gained independence at the end of World War II and Ho Chi Minh was installed as the premier of the provisional government.

However, not long afterwards, the nation became divided into north and south through the maneuvering of some powerful nations. Ho Chi Minh once again engaged in war with nations such as France and the United States in order to try to unify the people of Vietnam. However, as a result of many years in prison and war, Minh's health grew worse and he passed away without seeing his motherland unified. Seven years after his death, North Vietnam and South Vietnam were united to form the Socialist Republic of Vietnam.

Motivated by a love for his people, Ho Chi Minh spent his whole life for the independence and then the unification of his country. He is one leader respected by not only the Vietnamese people but the rest of the world.

호치민

베트남의 정치가, 1890년 5월 19일 ~ 1969년 9월 2일

사람을 사랑한 지도자 호치민은 1890년, 베트남의 작은 농촌 마을 킴 리엔에서 태어났습니다. 호치민이 태어났을 당시 베트남은 프랑스의 식민 지배를 받고 있었습니다.

학교에 다니면서 베트남 국민들이 핍박받는 모습을 보게 된 호치민은 농민들을 도와 시위에 참가했다가 퇴학을 당합니다. 그 후 자신이 조국을 위해 할 수 있는 일을 고민하던 호치민은 다른 나라를 여행하며 넓은 세상을 보고 배우기로 합니다. 그는 프랑스 배의 보조 요리사로 취직하여 세계 곳곳을 돌아다니면서 베트남의 실상을 알렸습니다.

이 일을 계기로 프랑스 경찰들에게 쫓기는 몸이 되고, 결국 30년 동안 조국으로 돌아오지 못하게 되었습니다. 비록 몸은 떨어져 있지만 호치민은 조국 독립을 위한 활동을 멈추지 않았습니다.

모든 준비를 마치고 51세에 베트남으로 돌아온 호치민은 본격적으로 공산주의 사상을 바탕으로 한 '베트남 독립 동맹(베트민)'의 활동을 시작합니다. 베트남 독립 동맹은 프랑스, 일본 등 강대국과 치열한 전투를 벌이며 베트남 독립에 앞장섭니다. 결국, 베트남은 제2차 세계 대전이 끝나면서 독립을 맞았고, 호치민은 임시 정부의 초대 주석으로 추대됩니다.

그러나 머지않아 베트남은 강대국의 힘에 의해 남과 북으로 갈리게 됩니다. 호치민은 다시 한 번 프랑스, 미국 등 강대국과 전쟁을 벌여 민족을 하나로 통일시키기 위해 노력했습니다. 그러나 오랜 감옥 생활과 전쟁을 겪은 호치민의 몸은 매우 약해져 있었고, 호치민은 조국의 독립을 보지 못한 채 눈을 감았습니다. 호치민이 죽고 난 지 7년이 지난 후 남베트남과 북베트남이 통일되어 '통일 베트남 사회주의 공화국'이 수립되었습니다.

사람을 사랑하는 마음으로 조국의 독립과 통일을 위해 평생을 바친 호치민은 베트남 국민들뿐 아니라 전 세계 사람들에게 존경 받는 지도자로 손꼽히고 있습니다.

이 책을 만든 사람들

글 · 이숙자

만화 스토리 작가로 왕성하게 활동하고 있습니다. 지금까지 고전, 명작, 과학, 논술, 경제 등 다양한 분야의 학습 만화 작업을 해 왔습니다. 현재는 어린이들이 닮고 싶고, 되고 싶은 인물 이야기를 쓰는 데 열중하고 있습니다. (firemecca@hanmail.net)

그림 · 스튜디오 청비

기발한 상상력을 바탕으로 새롭고 재미있는 콘텐츠를 만들어 내는 만화 창작 집단입니다. 어린이들이 책을 읽고 큰 꿈을 품기를 바라는 마음으로 즐겁게 작업하고 있습니다. 작품으로 『성철 스님』, 『아 다르고 어 다른 우리말 101가지』, 『반기문 유엔 사무총장의 꿈과 도전』 등이 있습니다.

번역 · 로라 김(Laura Kim)

미국 로스앤젤레스에서 태어났습니다. 뉴욕 주립대에서 교육학 석사 학위를 받았으며 미국 초등학교에서 교사로 일했습니다. 현재 한국에서 영어를 가르치며, 영어 교재 편집과 어린이 영어 교육 커리큘럼 제작에 힘쓰고 있습니다.

감수 · 김수희

연세대학교에서 역사를 전공했습니다. 이후 한국뿐 아니라 일본, 미국에서 한국어, 일본어, 영어를 가르쳐 왔으며 부모를 위한 영어교육용 책을 썼습니다. 영어교육채널 EBSe '엄마표 영어특강'에서 강의를 하며 홈스쿨, 알파벳과 파닉스, 다차원 테마 영어 수업 기법을 알리고 있습니다. 전국 각지에서 어린이 영어 교육에 대한 강연을 하며 창의적이고 열정적인 교수법으로 영어를 배우고자 하는 어린이와 부모들에게 많은 도움을 주고 있습니다.

Ho Chi Minh

Ho Chi Minh changed his names many times. Which of the following is not one of them?

a. Sinh Kung
b. Tat Thanh
c. Khiem

Answer: c

Contents

A Child with a Twinkle in His Eyes

*colony: A place that politically and economically belongs to another country, and has no rights as a nation.

Hey there, Sinh Cung! I'm your brother, Khiem.

He is so cute and tiny!

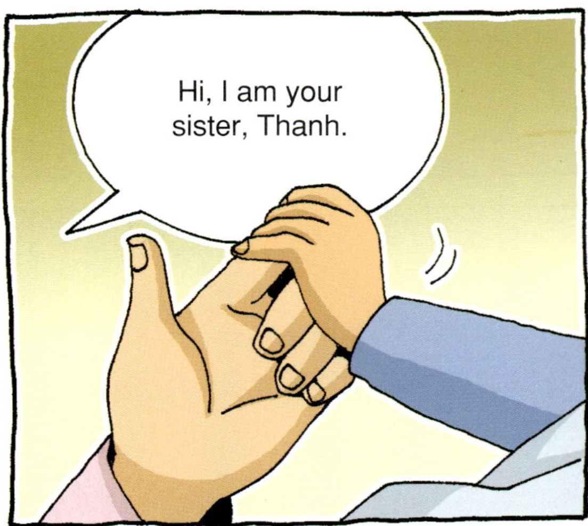

Hi, I am your sister, Thanh.

Goodness, I think Sinh Cung understood what I just said! He squeezed my finger.

Dad, do all babies have such an amazing twinkle in their eyes? His eyes are sparkling like stars!

His eyes do seem bright. He looks quite clever.
Sinh Cung, our people are going through a tough time, but I hope you will grow up to be someone who could save our country.
Sinh Cung was Ho Chi Minh's name when he was young. His father, Nguyen Sinh Sac, was a teacher at a small school in the village.
Hmm...
Two children didn't show up today. We are losing more and more of our students as time goes by. What should we do?

We can't really do anything about it. It's a world where everyone would rather go to French schools. Who would want their children studying Chinese characters when they need to learn French to get jobs?
Daddy!
What happened, child?
Sir, they say that my father might die soon!
What?
Was he dragged off by the French to work? Is that how he got hurt?
Even that might've been better. He was beaten until he was covered in blood. It's a miracle that he made it out alive.

CD1 Track 03 ► 
90% of us need to make a living by farming. We wish you wouldn't force us to leave our farms to do other work during the busy season!
Also, many are collapsing from malnutrition and overwork, so we demand that you provide us with enough food and time to rest!
What? How dare you complain? Shut your mouth and keep working!
You are the ringleader of this nonsense, right? You want to feel my boot, you savage colonial?

A-argh...
Cruel French pigs! How could they do this to you?
Daddy!
Don't cry, baby. He'll be alright.
That's terrible...
Dad, it makes me so sad.
Sinh Cung... He knows how to truly empathize with other people.

The Vietnamese had exceptional pride for their nation, and rejected the idea of foreign rule. This was especially true in Kim Lien, which was not only where Ho Chi Minh was born and raised, but also the center of the French colonialism resistance.

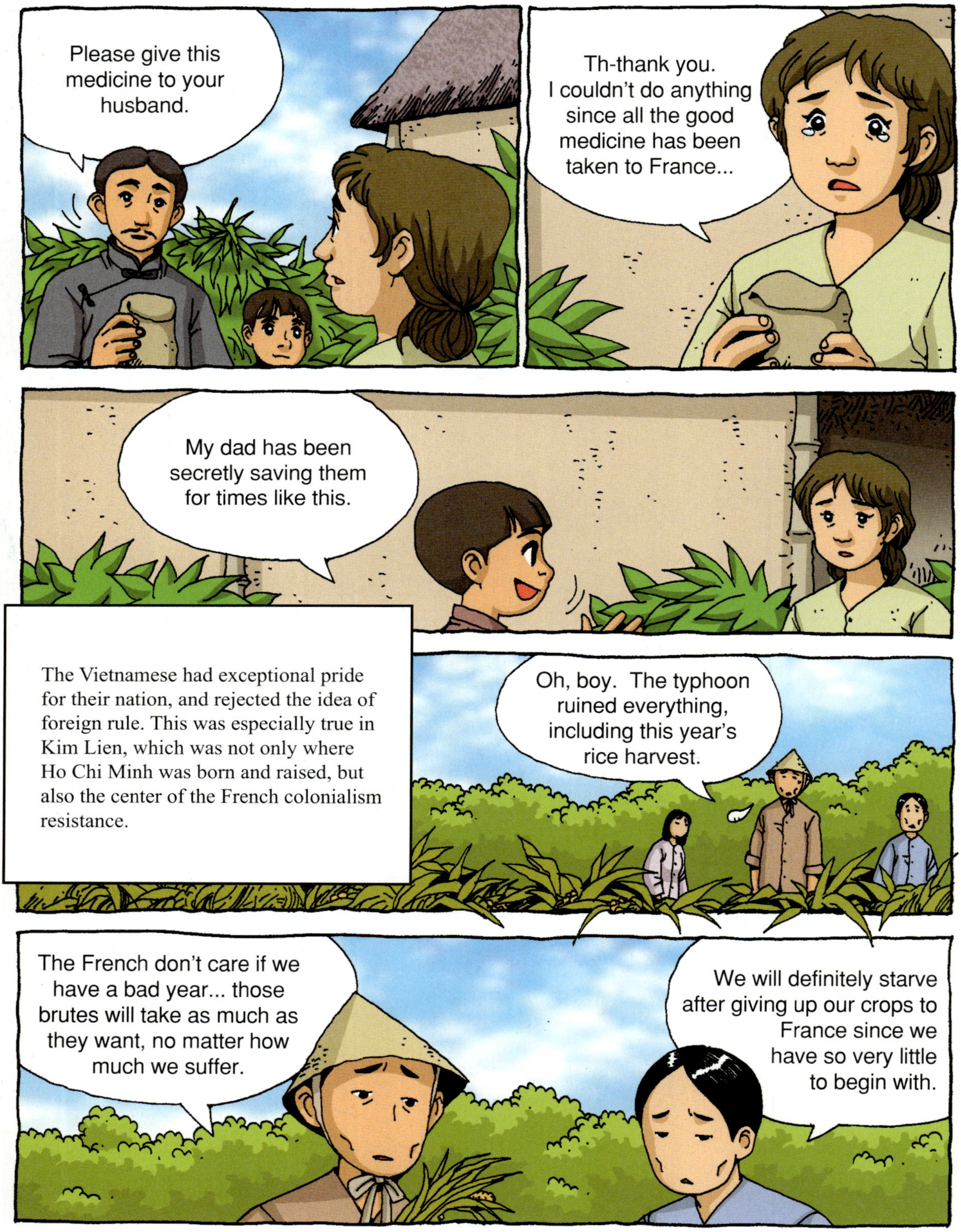

There are a lot of people in this village who are hiding their crops and not giving them up! Search all the houses and find all the crops!
No, please! That's for my newborn grandson!
Get out of my face, you old hag?
No, Mother!
Gaah!

*Betel palm: A tree that grows in warm countries that bears red fruits.

Cleans your teeth? Haha. Do you expect us to believe that when you have such horrible teeth?
Yuck! They're so gross!
Whatever. The real dirty ones are you, the French!
That's right! You are nothing but filthy thieves living in someone else's country!
What? Thieves? You just crossed the line!
Why are you taking my father away? The French kids started it!

My father didn't do anything wrong. Please let go of him!
Ouch!
Don't worry about me and go home, now!
You should have educated your kids better when you had the chance! How dare your son hit French children?!
Stop hitting my father! It's my fault!
I am sorry!
Like son like father! You need to learn to respect your betters. People like you two deserve a good beating.

Hmph. Another student had to drop out today.
That's so sad. I hate France!

This is all because we have lost our country. So, we need to become stronger, and become independent.
Sir, what can we do to make our country stronger?

That's a good question. First, you need to study diligently. After all, knowledge is power.
Yes, sir.
Now then, everyone, open your books and read what we learned yesterday.

Oh, goodness! How can we beat France if you cannot even remember what you learned yesterday?
In learn... learning... and st... st...

Chinese characters are just so difficult.
If no one can read it, then everyone will be punished!
Oh, no...
In learning and straightaway practicing, is there not pleasure also?
Good, Sinh Cung remembers how to read it. Go ahead and tell us the meaning.
This quote asks us if it is fun to study and then practice what we learn. But it's not really a question. It's just helping us see the fun in studying.
Whew, saved by Sinh Cung. He is the youngest, but learns the fastest.

When Ho Chi Minh was five years old, his family moved to the city of Hue, about 250 miles from his hometown. His father thought it would be better to move to a big city to continue with his studies and make it easier to take the civil services examination.

In the past, Vietnam was ruled by China. This meant everyone who wanted to become a government official in Vietnam had to study Confucianism and pass the civil services examination.

Ho Chi Minh's family had to walk through dangerous mountains full of thieves to get to their new home. It would have been a lot faster to take the boat, but they couldn't afford it.

But young Ho Chi Minh enjoyed the journey a great deal, because his father told him heroic stories from Vietnamese mythology and history.
Sinh Cung. Today, I will tell you about the person who founded Vietnam.
About 3,000 years ago, Lac Long Quan, a powerful dragon king from the sea, and Au Co, a mountain fairy, had 100 sons together.
I am a dragon lord and you are a fairy. We are from different worlds and I no longer think we belong together. Let's leave one another.
Then, take 50 of our sons and go to the sea. I will take the rest of our sons to the mountains.
One of the sons who went with the mother to the mountains later became Hung King, and he established a country in this land called Van Lang. Back then, Van Lang was a huge country stretching all the way to China.
Really? It's so surprising to learn that our people had such a big country!

That's right. Now you understand how great a people we are?

Darling, I don't want to risk being attacked by the thieves, so why don't we wait for other people and then go with them?

That's a good idea.

Mom, what do we do if the thieves show up?

Give me all you got!
I don't want to meet any thieves!

Thieves are not the only ones that you should be scared of. You never know when wild beasts might jump out at you.
No! I don't even want to think about it!

Now we are all going to die!
Don't say that! Are we really all going to die, Dad?
No, don't be silly. We can beat anything, beasts or thieves, so don't worry.
Whew, I guess I feel a little better. You are sure we can beat them, though, right?
Of course.
But how do we beat them? How?
Just don't let the fear of death get to you. If you can defeat your fear, then you can defeat anyone, no matter who or what they are.
Even the ones that are much stronger than us?
Sure. The reason we were able to defeat China's armies and win our freedom is because we didn't let our fear of death get to us.

Sinh Cung, there are many stories of brave heroes in our history. Let me tell you about the Trung sisters who fought bravely against the Chinese.
Vietnam was ruled by China for a long time. Born in a wealthy family in northern Vietnam, the Trung sisters dreamed about independence while watching Vietnam suffer under China.
Trung Nhi, Let's gather people to fight China.
That's a great idea, sis. But in order to get people to believe that women can lead them, we need to prove to them that we are brave and wise. Why don't we hunt a vicious tiger?
It was dangerous but after they killed a tiger, they went around Vietnam with the tiger skin and called for war against China's army in Vietnam.
Everyone. Let's all fight for our country's independence! We can defeat them if we do not fear death!

Let us fight, too. The Trung sisters went without any men to hunt a tiger and prove the strength of women.

The sisters led an army while sitting on top of an elephant, and regained castle after castle, until they drove the Chinese armies away and won Vietnam's independence. As the Trung sisters ruled Vietnam, they got rid of the tax laws China had created, making Vietnam a good country for their people to live in.

Hail, our Trung Queens!

But then the Chinese emperor sent vast armies to reconquer Vietnam.

This time, unfortunately, Vietnam lost. The Trung sisters could not handle the thought of the humiliation of being reconquered by China, so they took their own lives by throwing themselves in a river.

After hearing about the Trung sisters, who fought against China for independence, Sinh Cung felt proud to be Vietnamese, like the Trung sisters were.
They were so brave...
Sinh Cung, if you get scared and run away from your opponent, you will be defeated in the end. The Trung sisters knew that from the beginning.
We need the courage to fight while holding back our fear of death.
If I get scared and just run away before the fight, I'll get defeated?
I see.

Sinh Cung, are you still scared?
Ho Chi Minh took his father's words to heart. He deeply believed that if he didn't fear death, nothing could defeat him.
No, I am no longer afraid of anything! No matter how scary they are!
After Ho Chi Minh arrived at Hue, he slowly became interested in the things around him.
Wow, this place is a totally different world from where I used to live. There are so many amazing things here!
Gosh, try not to gawk, Sinh Cung. People will look down on us if they think we're from the hills.
I wonder what kind of people live there? It looks like a palace!

It's a no-brainer. I am sure French people live there.
Who knows, it could be one of those soulless Vietnamese who make a lot of money selling to the French.
See? I told you they would be French.

The French who live in our country have great lives, and the people who own the country are living like slaves! In what world does this make sense?

You are right. This does not make any sense.

Ho Chi Minh and his brother decided to sneak into one of the nearby army bases to watch French soldiers train.

Wow! I can't believe my eyes... how do they all move at exactly the same time?

Isn't it amazing? Sinh Cung, I heard that you have to have an army full of soldiers like these to have a strong country.

A strong army makes a strong country. The reason we became a French colony is because our army was weak.

I guess that means we have to make our army stronger than the French army, huh?
That's right. That way we can become independent.

Sinh Cung, make sure you take in everything you see right now, and try to remember how the soldiers train.
Okay, that sounds like a really good idea!
I want our country to become stronger, so other countries will leave us alone.

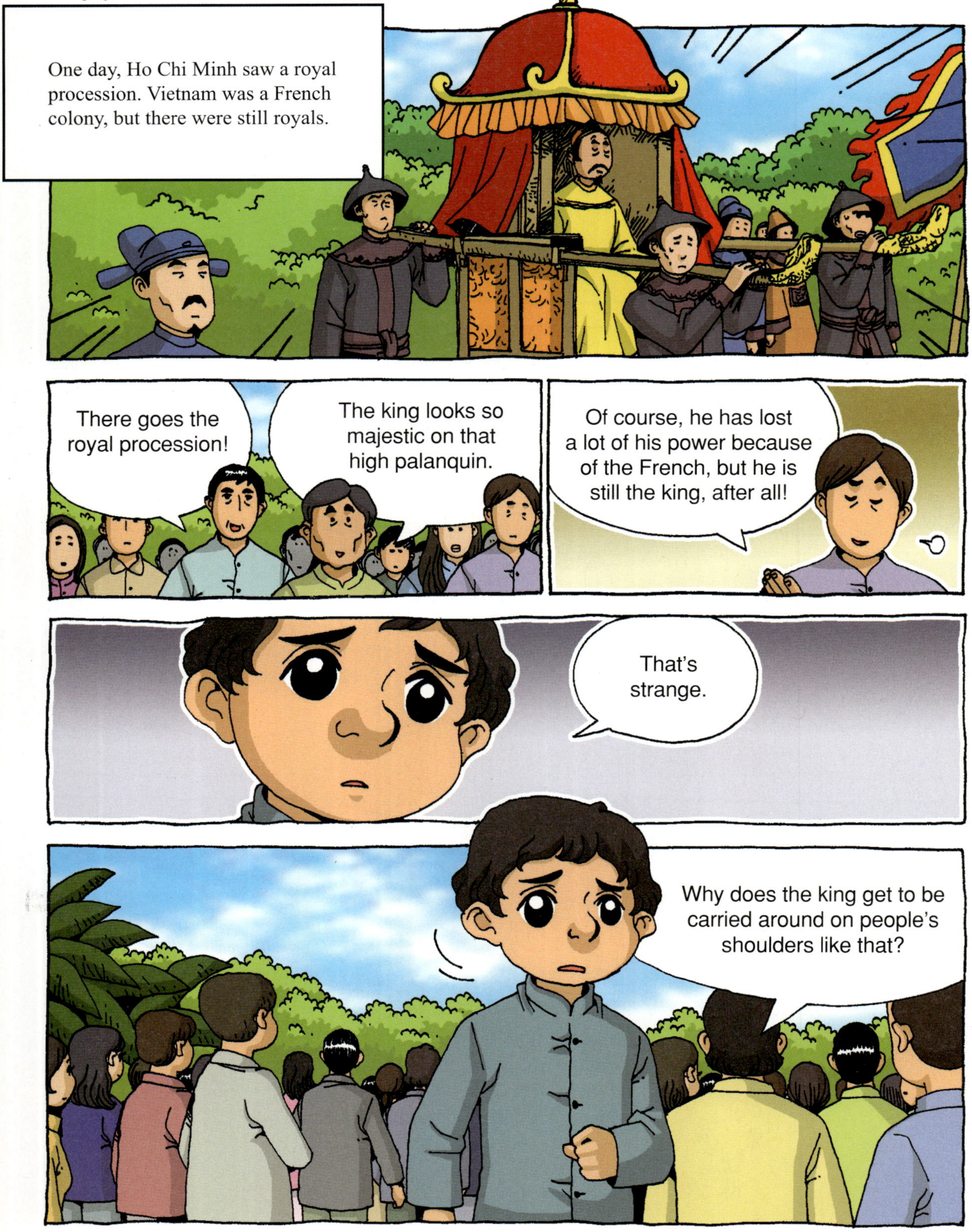

One day, Ho Chi Minh saw a royal procession. Vietnam was a French colony, but there were still royals.

There goes the royal procession!
The king looks so majestic on that high palanquin.
Of course, he has lost a lot of his power because of the French, but he is still the king, after all!

That's strange.

Why does the king get to be carried around on people's shoulders like that?

Mom, did the king hurt his leg?
What do you mean?
I just saw a royal procession, and the king was being carried in a palanquin.
That's not because he hurt his legs.
What? He is not hurt? Then why doesn't he walk with his own two feet?
Sinh Cung, people from the upper classes are supposed to ride in palanquins when they are going places.
Why? Why do they have to ride palanquins when their legs are fine?

There is no 'why.' That's just how things have always been!
I don't understand.
Why is it so strange for you to see people in the lower class serving the people in the upper class?
Class?
So, everyone thinks it's normal to be carried around above people's heads when they think you are important?

I wonder why people label each other high or low class, and I don't understand how they accept the way they are treated based on their class.

If I were king, I would definitely walk with my own two feet, and I'd greet everyone.

No matter what class the king comes from, it is not right to be carried around above people's heads. That will not help him learn how his people live!

A Time of Grief

CD1 Track 15 ▶

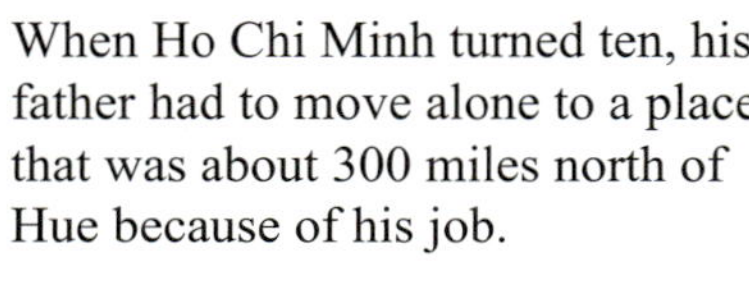

When Ho Chi Minh turned ten, his father had to move alone to a place that was about 300 miles north of Hue because of his job.

Tragically, Ho Chi Minh's mother passed away shortly after the difficult birth of her fourth child, Nguyen Sinh Nhuan.
Mom! You can't leave us like this when our father is not even here!
What about the baby? He hasn't even gotten to know you yet!
How are we supposed to raise him without you?
Sinh Nhuan, my poor baby brother...
Waaaah!
I know you are hungry. Why don't I take you out, since our big brother and big sister are busy with chores in the house? C'mere.

Excuse me, ma'am? It's me, Sinh Cung. Can my baby brother have some of your milk, please?
I can't believe a ten-year-old boy is taking care of a baby. You're such a good boy.
You poor thing.
Goodness, I just can't imagine how hard this must be for that young boy.

Ho Chi Minh had to beg for milk from house to house to feed his baby brother. Despite his efforts to save him, his baby brother died from illness before he could even turn one.
Sinh Nhuan! No, you can't leave us, Sinh Nhuan!
Kids? Are you okay?
Dad, what took you so long?
Dad!
Don't be so sad. I am sure your mother and your brother are now together in heaven.
Mom...

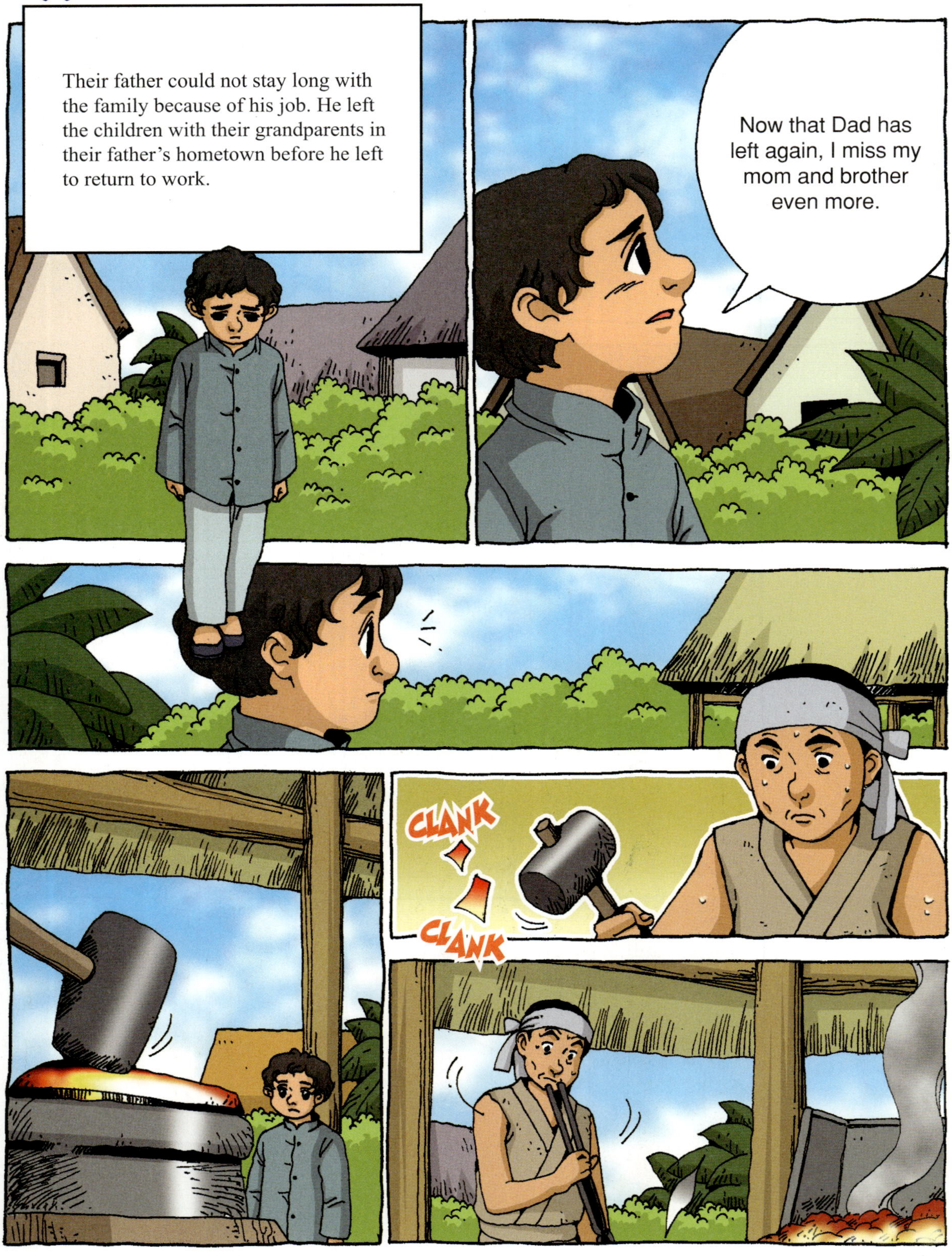

Their father could not stay long with the family because of his job. He left the children with their grandparents in their father's hometown before he left to return to work.

Now that Dad has left again, I miss my mom and brother even more.

CLANK

CLANK

*tempering: A method to make metal stronger by heating it in a fire and then cooling it by putting it in water or oil.

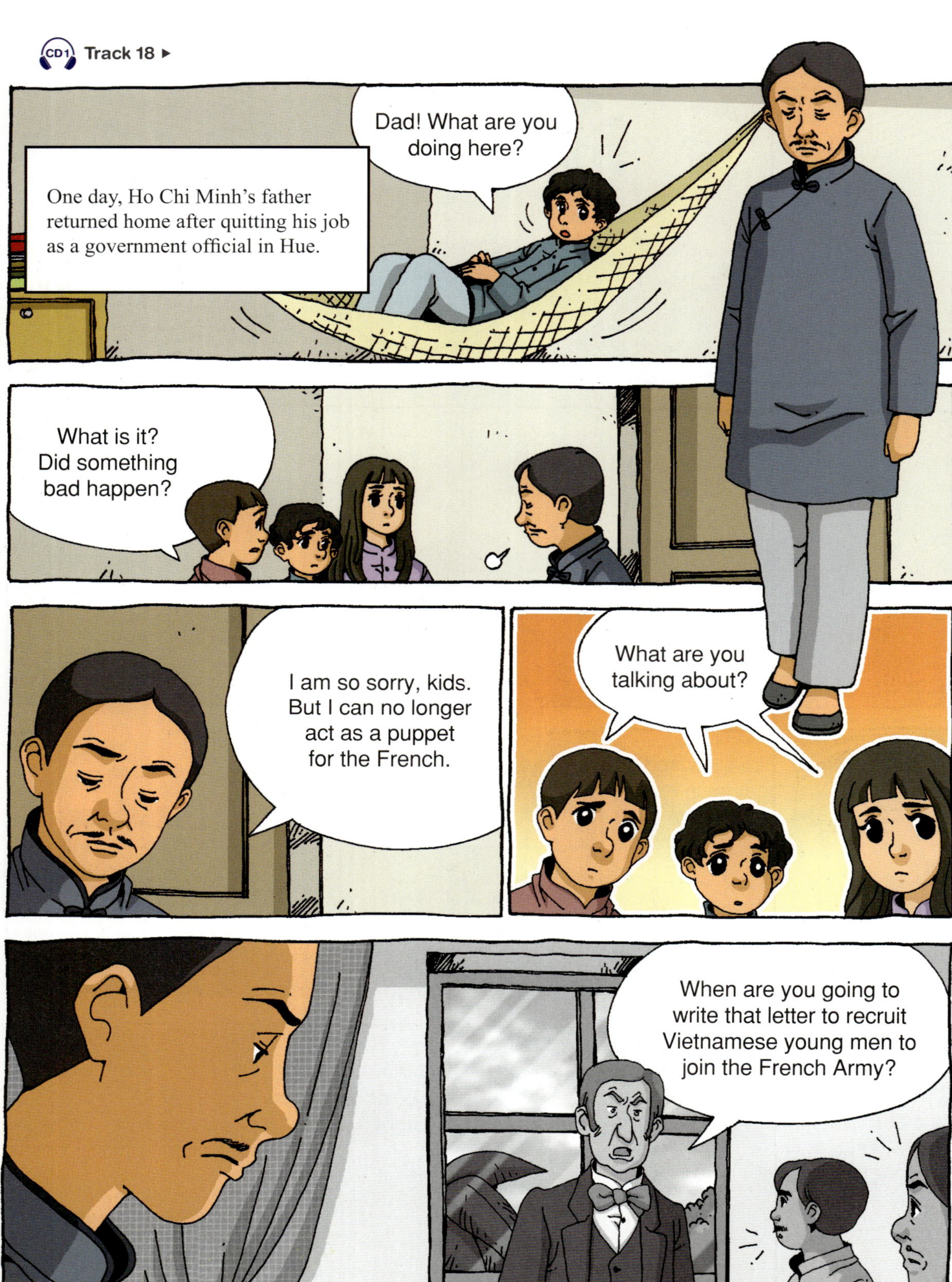
Dad! What are you doing here?
One day, Ho Chi Minh's father returned home after quitting his job as a government official in Hue.
What is it? Did something bad happen?
I am so sorry, kids. But I can no longer act as a puppet for the French.
What are you talking about?
When are you going to write that letter to recruit Vietnamese young men to join the French Army?

I would rather not write that letter.
What? Are you trying to disobey a French order? If you won't do the job, then you won't have a job! Now, do as I say and write the letter!
I can't believe working as a high-ranking official in the Vietnamese government is still just working for the French.
Hurry up and write everything I say. The title is "Dear young men of Vietnam who would love to serve their beloved country, France."
Um... sir? Would you please take a look at this?

Hey, just let it slide, will you? These are all my friends, and this was just a one-time thing that they asked me to do for them, so I just lent them a hand.

Ho Chi Minh's father opened up a school again upon his return to his hometown. Then, he changed his name to Nguyen Sinh Huy, meaning 'honorable.' He also gave Ho Chi Minh a new name, Nguyen Tat Thanh, which means 'accomplished.' Giving children new names when they became a young adult was a Vietnamese tradition.

One should not seek comfort, and should work for the people to make life better?
Ho Chi Minh's refusal to tolerate injustice from early in his life was hugely influenced by his father's teachings.
Those evil French! Why are they harassing us again? We are no threat to them...
Argh!!
Oh, no. If they don't stop then they are going to kill him!
Hey! You Vietnamese should watch and learn!

No! No, please, he's my son!
It's all my fault. Please have mercy on this old man and forgive us both. Please!
Why must such an elderly man get down on his knees and beg forgiveness from soldiers who are young enough to be his grandchildren?
Those animals should be ashamed. They are the ones who got drunk and picked a fight! That Vietnamese man did nothing!
I can't take this any longer.
I am going to go out there and fix it.
What are you talking about? Fix what?

Remember what Dad said?
Don't just stand there and watch injustice happen. Fight against it.
I know. But all we can do now is to study hard and build up our skills.
I think we should be studying more than just Chinese characters and Confucianism.
Why don't we go to learn French at the French school in Hue?
What? Where did that idea come from?
I feel like I have to know France well in order to beat the French. So don't you think I should start by learning the language first? I am sure Dad would give us permission.

Haha! Tat Thanh came up with a brilliant idea. We can't beat France by just studying Chinese Confucianism. Even Sun Tzu said that you need to know your enemy to beat your enemy.
Of course, you would first have to understand France!
When Ho Chi Minh turned 15, he entered a French school with his brother. At that time, the Vietnamese were forced to learn under the French education system so the writing style was changed to the French alphabet.
Hi, my name is Tat Thanh. Nice to meet you all.
Haha! What in the world is he wearing? What a country bumpkin!
Hey, farmer boy, what does your daddy do?
He's some teacher of a small Confucius school! Not that anyone still cares about old Chinese sayings.

Did you learn how to write "I'm a backwards farmer" in Chinese characters?
Hey, Tat Thanh, I bet you eat nothing but rice at your house. Am I right?
You guys are talking like you never eat rice.
Hahaha, I knew it!
What's so funny about eating rice?
Where did this kid come from? Even Vietnamese eat more bread than rice in Hue!
They do what!?

While these Vietnamese are saying they hate the French, they don't realize they are living more like the French every day by rejecting rice and drinking French wine.
But, if we continue this way, Vietnam will disappear!
We need to gain independence before that happens.
One day, Ho Chi Minh had the chance to visit his French classmate's house.
So, this is how the French live. It's like another world compared to how we Vietnamese live.

Are you done staring? Why don't you take a seat.
Even the chairs are completely different from what we Vietnamese have.
Sir, I'll take your bag for you.
Sir, I have prepared a warm bath and a change of clothes for you as well.
Sir, here is your snack.

What is this? He is being treated like he's some kind of prince.
We have more than 20 servants in our house. The old one out there, taking care of the garden, has been here the longest.

All the hard work is being done by the Vietnamese...

Hey, country boy!
How do you spend all day in a French mansion and still wear that dumb hat?
When are you going to lose this tacky hat, huh?

Get your hands off. I'm Vietnamese, and this hat is part of our tradition! But maybe you're too dumb to know that!

How dare you talk to me like that, you yokel!

Khiem...
You fool! Have you already forgotten why we are attending French school?

Instead of using all that energy to cause trouble, why don't you use it to study some more?
You are right. I should not forget why we are in this school. Getting into fights won't help me get rid of the French. Besides, fewer kids would mess with me if I started getting good grades.

Ho Chi Minh studied diligently, and did so well that he was invited into Quoc Hoc National School as a top student. Quoc Hoc was known as the best school with a French education system in Hue.

How can somebody be both a yokel and a nerd? Give me a break.

Hey, if you are jealous of him, just say so. Honestly, nobody here is as good as he is in French language, literature, culture, and philosophy.

I am not going to let you get to me. I am here for a reason.

Ho Chi Minh did not forget his Vietnamese roots while he learned about the French, their language, and their history. On top of his school studies, he studied on his own, reading many books on history and reformation, resistance and revolution. He never stopped worrying about Vietnam's future.

03 A Light Kindled in the Heart

I know how to speak French. I'll help translate your demands.

Thank you, young man.

Sure, that would be great.

I would like to present you with the Vietnamese farmers' demands. First, they would like a tax cut because they are struggling financially, and...

What?! How dare you make demands! Who do you think you are?

Get outta here!

TKWACK

Oh my gosh, Khiem's here!

Aaaaahhhh! Help me!
They are going to kill them!
Tat Thanh, run. Go, now!
Khiem, how could something like this happen? The farmers just wanted to live without losing everything they have. How could those thugs do this to innocent people?

Tat Thanh, you were part of the protest?
Yes, sir.
What were you thinking when you decided to participate in such a thing? You are barely more than a boy!
You think you are a farmer? You are a student who should be studying, not causing trouble!
How can you say that when you are Vietnamese, yourself?
What did you say?
All the farmers are living like slaves. But you and others like you are with the French, stealing from other Vietnamese and begging from the French. In what world could this be justified?

How dare you, you little brat! You are expelled from this school. You are nothing but a bad influence on the students!

Tat Thanh, I thought you were smarter than that. What a disappointment.

Actually, I am glad things turned out this way. Why would I want to do well in a school like this, only to become a puppet of the French in the local government?

But, where do I go now? I can't stay, but I can't go back home, either, since the police might be looking for me because of the protest...

Ho Chi Minh was expelled from Quoc Hoc because he participated in the farmers' protest. The trouble did not end there, however. His father, his brother, and even his sister scattered to avoid the police.
He didn't hear from his family for a long time. When he eventually received a message, all it said was that his father had died alone on the streets.
The tragedy of Vietnam began long before Ho Chi Minh was born. It started with the attack of the French army in August, 1858. France started the war, claiming that the Vietnamese royalty had murdered a French missionary, but that was only a convenient excuse for the invasion.

At first, the French took over southern Vietnam in order to colonize it in 1862. Then they continued to take over other countries near Vietnam, such as Cambodia and Laos. Finally, in 1885, they pushed into northern Vietnam and colonized it as well.

The French divided Vietnam into three parts, naming them: Tonkin (Northern Vietnam), Annam (Central Vietnam), and Cochinchina (Southern Vietnam), and then they brutally exploited the three regions. European powers*, at the time, were eager to colonize small countries in Asia, Africa, and South America.

*power: A country that has a strong military and a large territory.

The French made numerous ports and railways all over Vietnam to make it easier for them to bring the country's resources back to France.

You better not slack off! Hustle!

I can't believe we have spent years here working like slaves for the French. We should be farming back home!

Vietnam's rice paddies, rubber tree forests and coal mines were all taken by the French.

What's the point of working? The French take everything we find.

The Vietnamese had to work like slaves in rice paddies, forests and mines, all for very little pay. The situation was especially bad in the rubber tree farms in the south, where many workers died due to illness or physical abuse.

I feel dizzy. It's long after lunch time, but they aren't giving us any food.

Do I look like a nurse? Don't be such a crybaby!

Hey, you. Is this all you got?

I am not feeling well.

POW

Also, the Vietnamese had to offer nearly all their harvested food, and had to pay high interest whenever they borrowed money.

I have no idea what I am going to do about the harvest this year. The drought ruined all my crops.

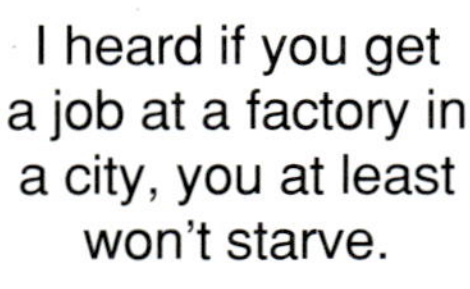
I heard if you get a job at a factory in a city, you at least won't starve.

Farmers went to the cities to find jobs, but they didn't do much better in the cities. The pay was better, but the taxes were very high.

I don't understand. I am making a lot more money compared to when I was working on the farm, but living is tougher here...

That's because prices are higher in the city.

These days, people say ten dollars on the farm is like one dollar in the city.

This is all because of France. They are charging way too much money for the necessities. We'll never get away from this life.

The price for salt went up again? That's ridiculous!

It's because of French taxes. If we didn't raise the price, we wouldn't make any money.

This is driving me crazy. I can't just stop using salt.

No matter how hard I work, all I get is debt.

We don't have a future anymore. How long do we have to put up with living like this?

I feel completely helpless. I spent so much time studying the French, just to prepare myself to fight against them, but there is still nothing I can do here.
Track 30

After being expelled from Quoc Hoc National School, Ho Chi Minh traveled around Vietnam, working odd jobs. The situation was bad no matter where he went. The French exploited the Vietnamese so they could live comfortably while the Vietnamese were barely surviving each day.
Do you love Vietnam?
Of course. Why do you ask?
Can you keep a secret?
Sure, what is it?
I am going to go abroad. I feel that if I could visit international powers and learn their ways, I think it'll help me figure out a way for Vietnam to have a better future.

Ho Chi Minh got a job as a cook's assistant on a French cargo ship that planned to sail around the world.

The only things you could do on this ship are menial jobs, like helping the cook. You need to handle all the work by yourself, including dish washing, ingredient preparation, floor mopping.
I assure you that I can do anything you'd want me to do.
Hmm. You look a bit skinny, but you do look bright enough.
Whew, I am so glad that I got a job.
What's your name anyways? You are not somebody the police are after, are you?
N-no! My name is 'Ba.' Please check the document, it's on there.

I don't know how many times I have changed my name because of the police.
Ho Chi Minh was being chased by the police after taking part in several farmers' protests. In order to evade the police, he used over 169 fake names. Even the widely known Ho Chi Minh is a fake name.
To Thanh and Khiem, I am leaving Vietnam to learn about the world. Please take care of yourselves, and I will see you when I get back in five years.
In June of 1911, Ho Chi Minh left Vietnam by ship from Saigon, a southern port city. Nobody knew then that it would be 30 years before he would return.

04 A Young Colonial

During the three years that Ho Chi Minh worked on the ship, he had the chance to visit countries in Europe, Asia, Africa, and South America. As he visited those places, he saw many people of color being colonized by European Caucasians. All the nations that lost their independence were going through as much pain as the Vietnamese were.

In 1914, after three years of working on the ship, Ho Chi Minh began living in England. He worked numerous odd jobs, including working as a janitor, a boiler repairman, and a cook's assistant in a hotel kitchen. His life was hard, working constantly just to survive.

It's unbearably hot in this boiler room, but it's better than freezing in the snow outside. This is so exhausting. But I guess it's no worse than how our people have been living for the past 50 years...

It really is difficult to learn about the world like this.

Tat Thanh. Metals only get stronger through tempering.

That's right. I have to keep my hopes up, especially through difficult times like this. One day, all of this will have been worthwhile!

Whoa, who threw away perfectly fine food?

I should keep it aside and give it to poor people.

What are you doing, going through the trash?

How could you call this trash? Why would you waste food like this? There are a lot of people out there who've never seen this kind of food and would be glad to have this.

How do you eat someone else's leftovers? It's disgusting.

I don't think it's disgusting at all. What's truly disgusting are those people who would waste food.

Ho Chi Minh read anything he could get his hands on whenever he had time. Any British newspaper, magazine or book had a vast amount of knowledge that he had never seen in Vietnam.

Reading is all you do when you have free time. Why don't you eat lunch?

I am okay. I had some of the leftovers.
Why do you read so much, anyways?

I want to know and understand more about the world. That's the only way that I can help my country.
I have no idea what you're talking about.
Of course you wouldn't get what I am saying. You have never lost your country before.
But the more I read, the more I can see how I am not doing enough. I need to take action to really help my country...
That's it!
Yikes! What? What's it?

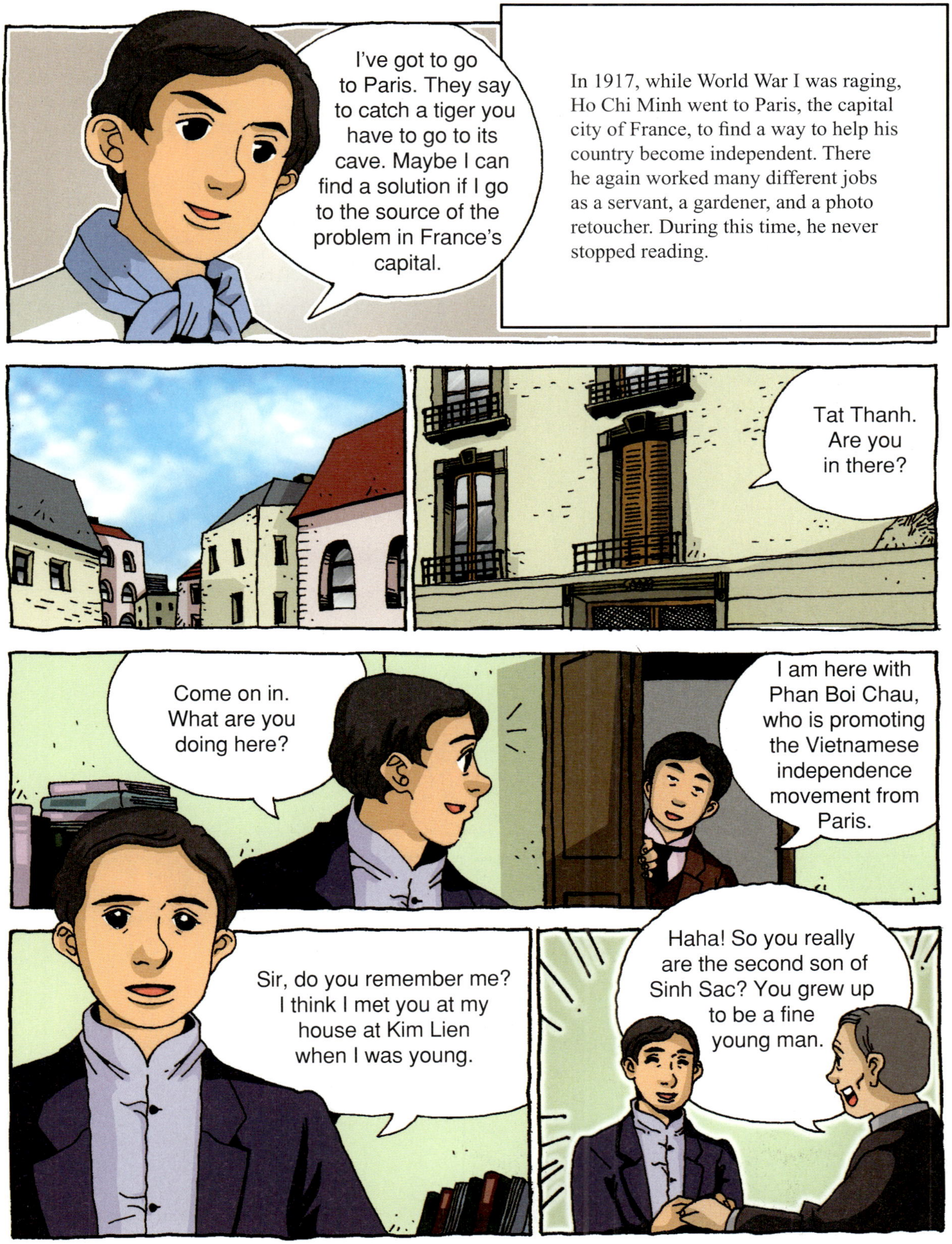

In 1917, while World War I was raging, Ho Chi Minh went to Paris, the capital city of France, to find a way to help his country become independent. There he again worked many different jobs as a servant, a gardener, and a photo retoucher. During this time, he never stopped reading.

For the first time in years, Ho Chi Minh got to speak to other vietnamese people. These were independence activists working secretly in Paris. Together, Ho Chi Minh began to become a part of the independence movement in earnest.

Tat Thanh. Are you familiar with the principal of national self-determination that America's President Wilson spoke of?

All people have the right to decide their fate and maintain their independence. This is the principle of self-determination!

Yes, it was inspiring for us to hear it.

I think so, too. Speaking of which... there is going to be a peace conference at Versailles. It shall be a gathering of all the representatives of the countries that achieved victory in the war.

We can't miss this golden opportunity! I need to write a proposal to free Vietnam and present it to them.

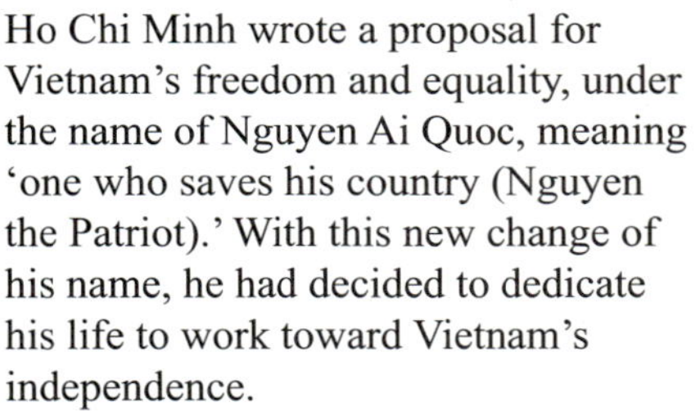

Ho Chi Minh wrote a proposal for Vietnam's freedom and equality, under the name of Nguyen Ai Quoc, meaning 'one who saves his country (Nguyen the Patriot).' With this new change of his name, he had decided to dedicate his life to work toward Vietnam's independence.

I insist that France guarantees the Vietnamese people's freedom and from this day forward ban forced labor.

I must meet the Allied representatives. The fate of Vietnam depends on it!

In January of 1919, Ho Chi Minh went to the Palace of Versailles to attend the Versailles Peace Conference, where all the Allied Powers' representatives were gathering. But before he could even submit his proposal, he was kicked out by the guards.

Stop trying to waste everyone's time! Get lost!

No one was willing to listen to the demands of a weak country like Vietnam. The Versailles Peace Conference was a meeting where the world's powers who had won World War I gathered to divide up the colonies.

Ho Chi Minh handed out his writings to people on the street and sent his essays to the French president, politicians and the press, and French society began to take notice of him. Soon, Ho Chi Minh became a man who received the attention of both the French and the Vietnamese.

I can't believe I thought I could get their help to establish our independence... I was foolish. We need to regain our freedom on our own.

The Vietnamese Want Independence!

France Needs to Leave Vietnam!

All People Have the Right to Decide Their Own Fate!

A Young Vietnamese Man Cries out for Liberty!

*Lenin: A politician from the USSR. He created and led the Communist Party and directed the Russian Revolution.
*USSR: current-day Russia, along with around a dozen other nearby countries.

Socialism was an idea that was gaining popularity in Europe. Ho Chi Minh was drawn to its ideas which said an individual owned nothing, but rather everything was shared by all the people. Everyone then used their society's resources to create a country that everyone would be politically and economically equal.

After having seen how the French abused the Vietnamese, he dreamed of a country where everyone was equal and he believed that only Socialism could help Vietnam achieve this.

Ho Chi Minh began to write, print and distribute a newspaper called Le Paria, meaning 'The Outcast.' He dedicated his message to the workers and farmers of the lower classes.

It says here that we, the workers and farmers, have to work together to make independence possible.

This person knows exactly how it feels to be exploited and repressed as colonized people.

As Ho Chi Minh's influence spread to other colonized countries, the police surveillance intensified, forcing him to move and change jobs to avoid arrest.

For Independence

*Indochina: Eastern part of the Indochinese peninsula that the French occupied from the late 19th to the early 20th centuries. Now, the region referred to as Indochina is made up of three countries: Vietnam, Laos, and Cambodia.

Ho Chi Minh held nothing back as he criticized the French in front of the gathered Europeans. Then he insisted that other European countries support the independence of Vietnam and other colonized countries.
It is not only the Vietnamese who are suffering as a French colony, but the people in other colonized nations are all leading miserable lives.
We French Socialists are making efforts to help. However, it is not an easy problem.
Please wait until I am finished speaking.
Hmph.
Hahaha!
Everyone, please keep it down.
I believe the Socialist Party should take an interest in the liberation of colonized nations. Please, I am asking you to send our comrades to Indochina and support them. Comrades, please, help us!

Ho Chi Minh's speech continued the following day and he was also reported about in major French newspapers, further spreading the news.

All Attention on Young Man from Asia!

Only having been in France for three years, and a novice in politics, the young man gave a speech in front of prominent leaders. On top of that, he started his speech confidently, demanding everyone give him their full attention.

Hmph. We'll see about this later.
The French Socialist Party then split into the Communist Party and the Socialist Party. Ho Chi Minh chose to be part of the Communist Party, which took a step beyond socialism and insisted that workers and farmers lead a revolution to eliminate the social classes.

Now the French police are following me everywhere I go. I guess they are trying to stop me from participating in the independence movement by watching my every move?
I don't like this. I really have to come up with a plan to get rid of him.
He was out until late last night meeting people. Now, where is he going so early in the morning?

Dear Minister of Colonization,
I noticed that you have appointed me a secretary from the police. I don't know how to truly show my appreciation, for he has been following me everywhere to see to my needs. However, I do not want to waste workers' tax money. Please take back your secretary.

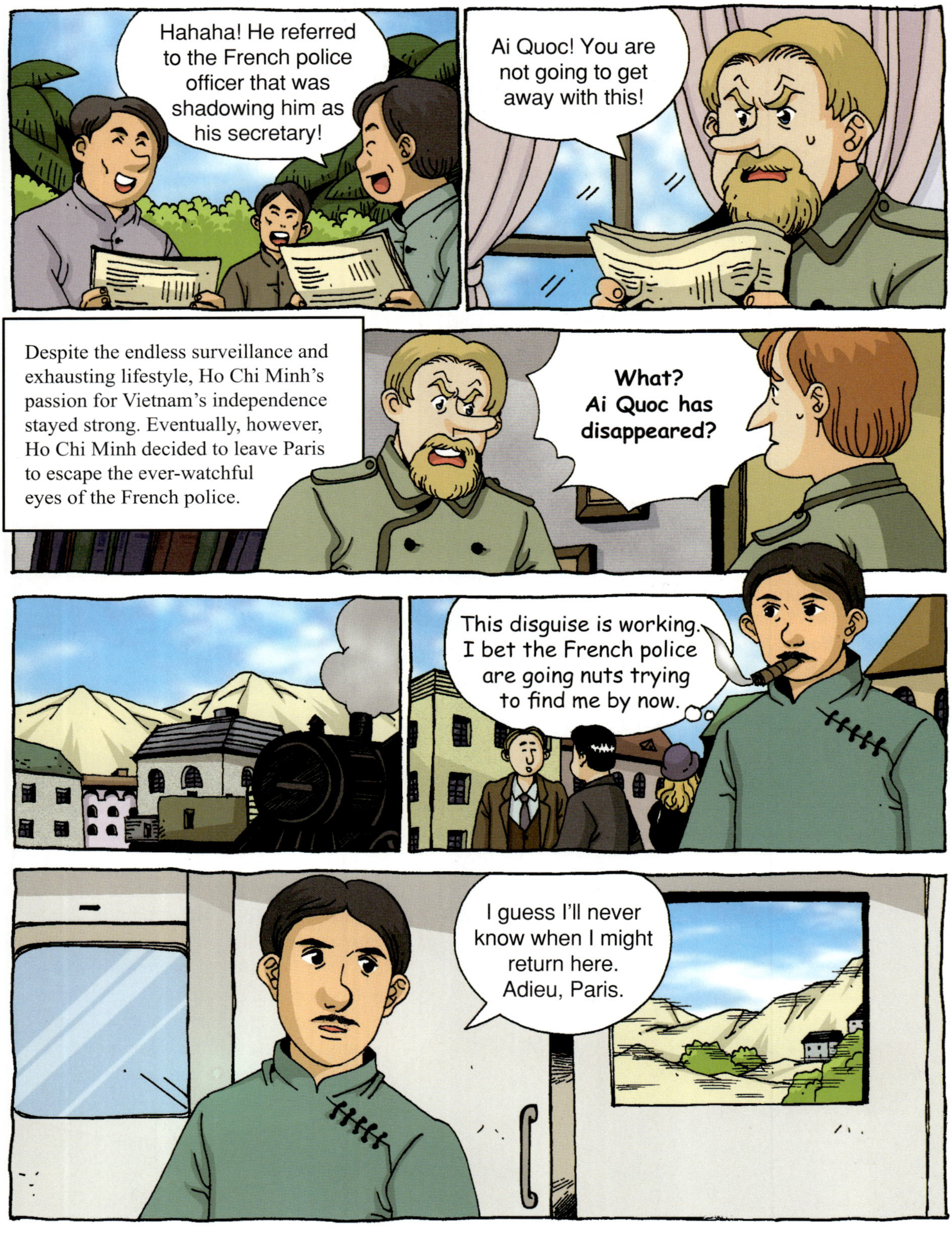

Despite the endless surveillance and exhausting lifestyle, Ho Chi Minh's passion for Vietnam's independence stayed strong. Eventually, however, Ho Chi Minh decided to leave Paris to escape the ever-watchful eyes of the French police.

Ho Chi Minh went to Moscow in the USSR and took various classes on leading communist revolutions, such as 'How to train an army', 'How to create newspapers and magazines' and 'How to gather people and educate them.'

It's very important to have a strong army to fight against the French. I especially need to make sure I learn ways to train our future army.
Sinh Cung, training a strong army is the way to make the country stronger. So, take a good look.

I've got to hurry up and bring everything I've learned here to the Vietnamese...

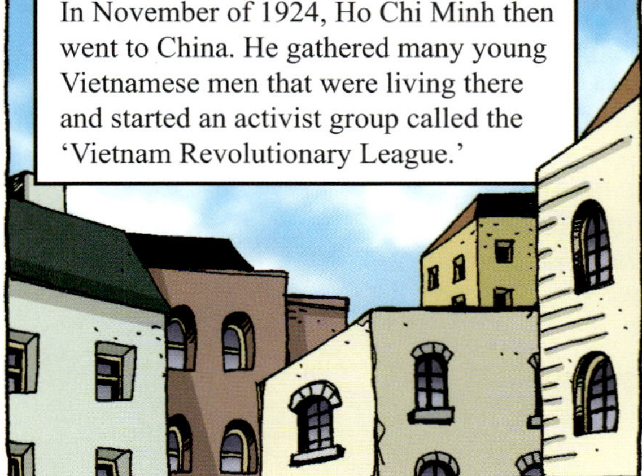

In November of 1924, Ho Chi Minh then went to China. He gathered many young Vietnamese men that were living there and started an activist group called the 'Vietnam Revolutionary League.'

Everyone, nothing is worse than losing one's own country.

The young men who learned from Ho Chi Minh went back to Vietnam to spread his teachings. However, since he was still being pursued by the French police. Ho Chi Minh traveled around Hong Kong, the USSR, Germany, and France to evade the police.

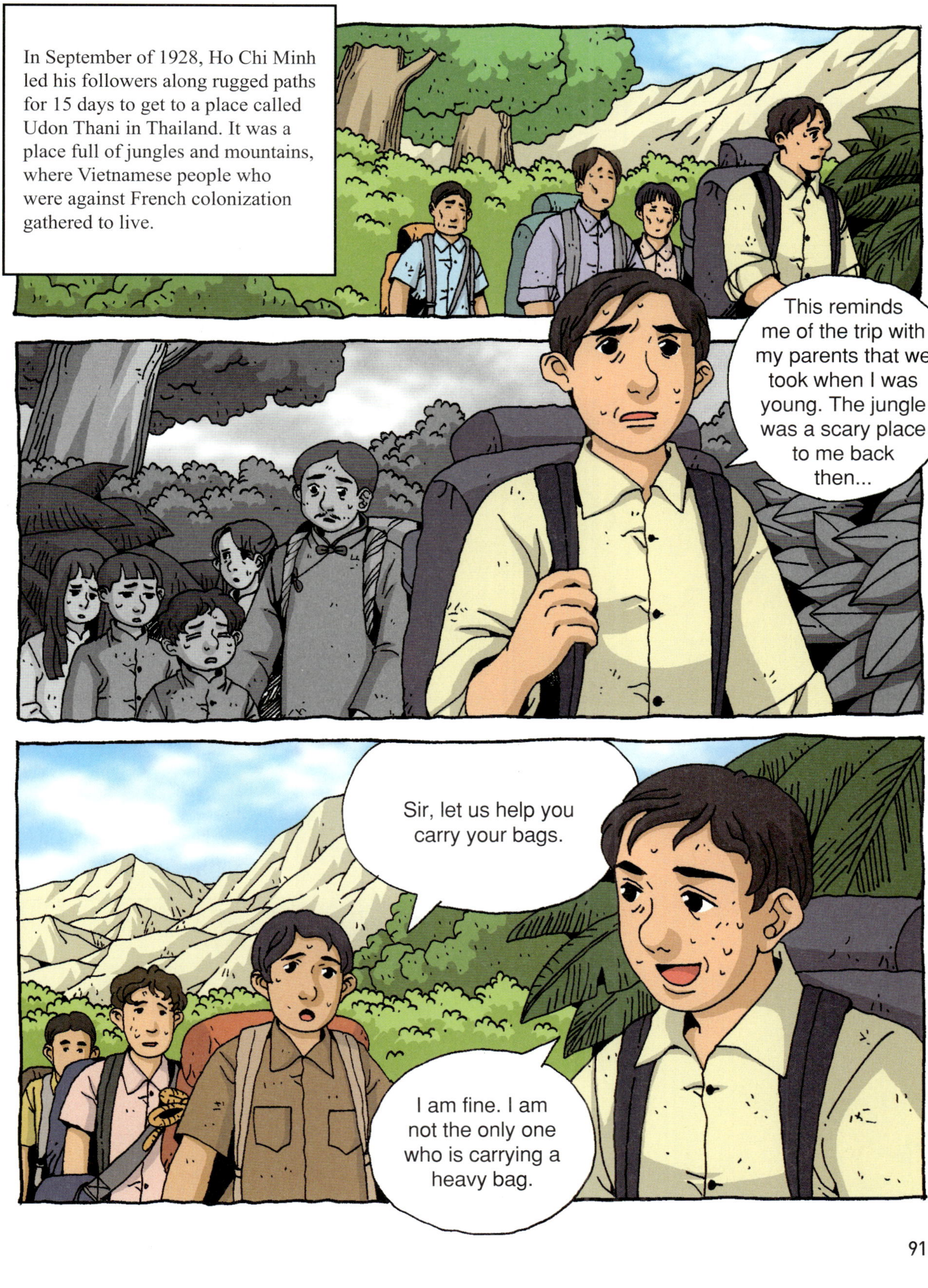

In September of 1928, Ho Chi Minh
led his followers along rugged paths
for 15 days to get to a place called
Udon Thani in Thailand. It was a
place full of jungles and mountains,
where Vietnamese people who
were against French colonization
gathered to live.

Once he arrived at Udon Thani, he helped the locals by farming and digging wells. He even opened a small school in one part of the village to teach children and adults that never received a formal education.
He is out in the field again. He's like a kind next-door neighbor rather than a world-traveling schoolteacher.
You're here!
You little rascal! You're covered in mud! Let's go to the stream and get you cleaned up!
Ho Chi Minh had a special place in his heart for children, granting any favor asked by a child, and singing them lullabies at night. The Vietnamese settlers called him 'Uncle Ho.'
Haha, he has kicked off his blanket in his sleep again. Keep his body warm to avoid getting sick.
Thank you!

*treason: To betray one's country either by attacking it or supporting a foreign country's attempts to attack it.

There are conflicts and fighting between Vietnamese and Chinese young men. There are already people who got hurt.

Uncle Ho, it would be dangerous to go to Hong Kong now. You know that France has sentenced you to death.

Oh, I am sorry. I had forgotten about that. I just thought...

It's okay. Let's go now. Our country's independence comes first, even before my life.

Ho Chi Minh was the only one who could resolve the conflict among the young men. He headed to Hong Kong without any delay.

Everyone has scattered. The situation is a lot worse than I had heard. First, gather all the representatives of the groups involved. We need to meet in one place.

Understood.

Everyone, we have got to work together if we are going to make Vietnam independent.
You just won't stop, will you?
Did you just hear comrade Ai Quoc? If the conflict continues...
I heard him. Who are you to lecture me? You mind your own business.
Comrades, we are leaders. We should be setting examples for others to follow. How will we ever win our independence if we continue fighting amongst ourselves like this?
W-well...
It's all our fault. I take a large part of blame as well. But the most important thing now is not whose fault it is. Please think of our people back home. They are suffering as we sit here arguing.

Of course, you are right. For Vietnam's liberation, we must work together.
Okay, let's put our arguments behind us and work together.
I agree, as well.
Ai Quoc truly knows how to talk to people. He can resolve even the most serious conflict.
Let's take this chance to unify all of the youth organizations and make an official communist party.
That's a fine idea. But what would we name this party?
Hmm. How about our country's original name, 'Vietnam,' since France has forbidden us to use it?

We will divide Vietnam into three parts and refer to the northern part as Tonkin, the central part as Annam, and the southern part as Cochinchina. If they keep using the name Vietnam, it'll only make the Vietnamese want to be independent again!
France not only took Vietnam's independence and wealth, it even took Vietnam's name away as it colonized the country. Ho Chi Minh decided to take back the name for the people of Vietnam.

'Vietnam' sounds perfect!

Thank you, Uncle Ho! We have gotten our name back because of you.
In February of 1930, Ho Chi Minh unified all the separate youth organizations and formed the 'Communist Party of Vietnam.' This step gathered the people's strength and prepared them for a path to found a new country under Ho Chi Minh's direction.

06 Fighting for Liberty

The Communist Party of Vietnam encouraged the people to become more aggressively resistant to France. On September 12, 1930, one of the biggest rebellions occurred, with about 6,000 farmers taking part.

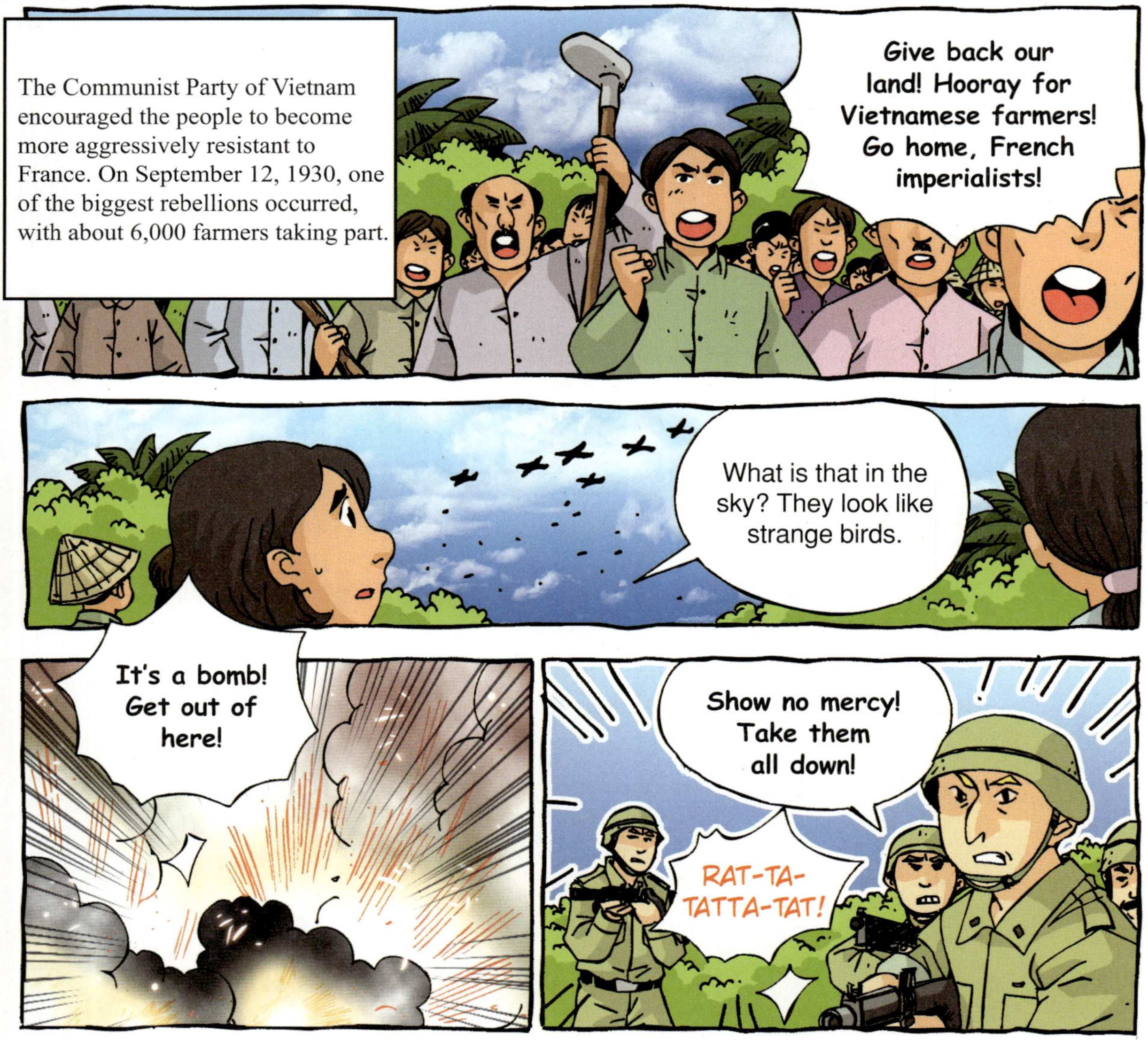

The French army dropped bombs and shot down thousands of weaponless farmers who were marching in protest. That night, blood flowed like rivers and bodies piled up like mountains in the village.

*Indochinese Communist Party: A new name to represent the Indochina peninsula, which included Laos in the north and Cambodia in the south.

How can they lose sight of the fact that our country's independence is the most important thing!

Yes, let's change the name of the party. How about we have comrade Tran Phu lead the party this time?

How could this happen? How could the Communist Party reject you?

It is not important. The new leader, Tran Phu, is both smart and a new revolutionary, so we should give him a chance.

In March, 1931, Tran Phu called a meeting of the Indochinese Party while trying to avoid French surveillance. At the time, Ho Chi Minh was living by himself in a shabby apartment in Hong Kong.

It's too bad that Ai Quoc couldn't join us today.

What are those shadows outside?

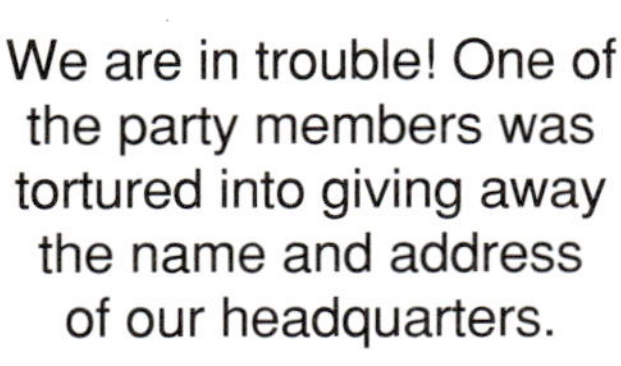

The secret gathering that was led by Tran Phu was caught by the French police. All the leading members of the party were arrested and executed, and the Indochina Party collapsed.

I think you are mistaken. My name is Wang and I am Chinese.
Don't think you can fool me. We know who you are.

Ho Chi Minh was arrested and jailed in Hong Kong. While imprisoned, his life was miserable. He had to endure eating spoiled food and endless torture.
Arrgh!

I-I can't die like this. I need to live through this... for my country... and for the people of Vietnam.

Ha! I guess I am not the only one in this cell. This little bug is also with me.

What do you think, bug? Do you think I will make it out of here alive? Should I have hope? Yes, that's right. I shouldn't lose hope...

Hey, stand up. The doctor is here. Step out, now!

This person has tuberculosis. Since he can be contagious, he needs to be quarantined while he is treated.

Comrade, I am a member of the Communist Party. I am here to save you.

What?!

Freed from prison and eager to help his people, Ho Chi Minh ignored the doctor's warning about needing to rest, and started working again. First, he redirected the Communist Party and once again started to speak out to the Vietnamese people.

On January 28, 1941, Ho Chi Minh returned to Vietnam, after 30 years of exile. Ho Chi Minh and his people had to walk endlessly along steep cliffs and through dense forest to get to a safe haven called 'Pac Bo Cave' located in the northern part of Vietnam.

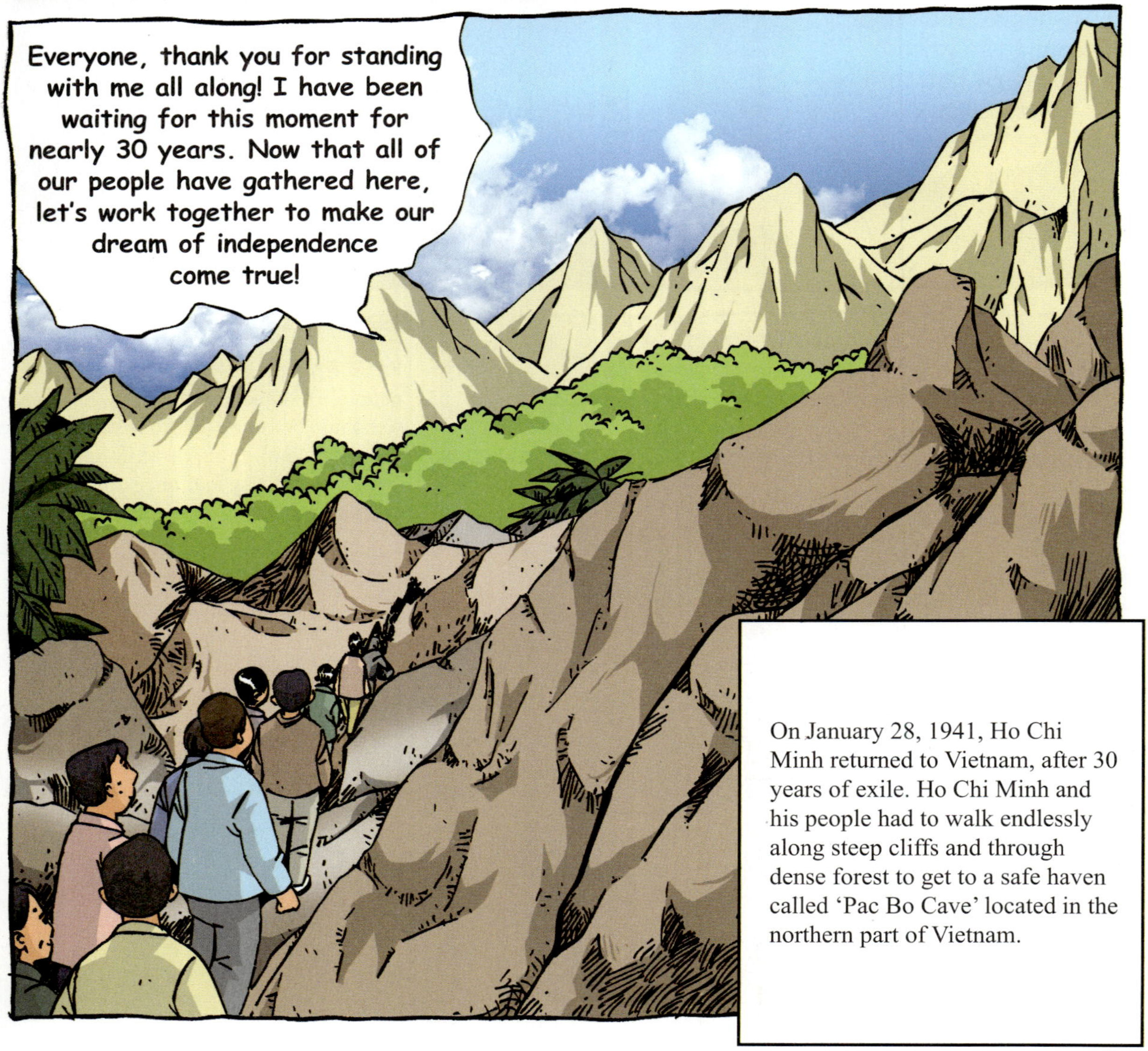

It was at this time that he decided to use the name Ho Chi Minh, which means 'enlightened will.' The name represented his determination to bring about the independence of Vietnam. Whenever he had time, he sat outside the cave next to the stream and he wrote *Viet Nam Doc Lap (Vietnam Independence)* newsletter, using a big flat rock as a desk. Many farmers who have read his writing came to the Pac Bo Cave, and ultimately Viet Minh, the League for the Independence of Vietnam, was formed here.

Shortly after Germany occupied France, Germany's ally*, Japan, sent their army into Vietnam. At first, the Vietnamese welcomed the Japanese armies thinking they would help free Vietnam. Unfortunately, the Japanese armies exploited the Vietnamese even worse than the French had.

*ally: A person or country that has decided to work together with a partner to benefit each other.
*castor bean: A tropical plant whose beans can be used to create an oil used for industrial lubrication.

Eat the dirt for all I care! We need castor bean oil to make more weapons!
We have two enemies now. And we are still too weak to fight against them. What should we do?
Ho Chi Minh decided to accept America's help to attack France and Japan. At the time, America was fighting against both Germany and Japan.
Welcome to the resistance.
Here are the six pistols that you requested.

Thank you. Here is the confidential document we obtained from the Japanese military.
We will soon send you medicine, two-way radios and more weapons.
After getting weapons with American support, Ho Chi Minh didn't hold back in starting an aggressive campaign to win Vietnam's independence from both France and Japan, using violence to fight violence.
We need to deal with both France and Japan at the same time. Of course, I am not going to say it's going to be easy. However, we do have an advantage. This is our land.
Ho Chi Minh was right. We know our land better than they do, and we can use it to defeat them!
Argh! Why won't they stand and fight? How can we fight them when they ambush us from the jungle, only to hide again in a flash?

I have heard Japan has been defeated by the French and the British. It's only a matter of time until they leave our land.
That's good news. But it's also bad news that France won.

That's right. Once the Japanese army leaves this land, France will again try to take over Vietnam.

Sir, how do we defeat the French when they return?

There is only one thing we can do! We must take over the capital city, Hanoi, once the Japanese armies have left and before France returns!

On August 15, 1945, World War II came to an end. Much like Ho Chi Minh had said, the Japanese declared their surrender to America.
Sir, it would be a piece of cake to go into Hanoi now. Just let us know when we should go.

We shouldn't rush. We will let the professional soldiers drive out the rest of the Japanese resistance and get the emperor of Vietnam to surrender as well.

That night, Hanoi was covered in darkness.

Will we have peace again once Japan and France leave us alone? I really want all of this to be over.

BANG BANG
Wh-what's that?

Everyone, listen up!
We are Vietnamese fighting for our independence. Soon, our soldiers will enter Hanoi!

Re-really? Then we'll become independent?
Yes! Take your places at our side and join us!

Grab anything you can find as a weapon and meet back here.
Hey, over there! A Japanese officer is escaping!

Seize him!

P-please! Japan has already lost the war. Please, just spare my life.

We were royalty in name only. We had no power. Do what you think is right.

Everyone, we have won! Let's all gather in the square.

Finally, we have arrived at Hanoi. Look at all these waves of red welcoming us!

Following the directions of Ho Chi Minh, the Viet Minh were able to take over most of the north-central part of Vietnam and make a triumphal entry into Hanoi. After long years of being colonized, they were able to rebuild their nation as the 'Democratic Republic of Vietnam.'

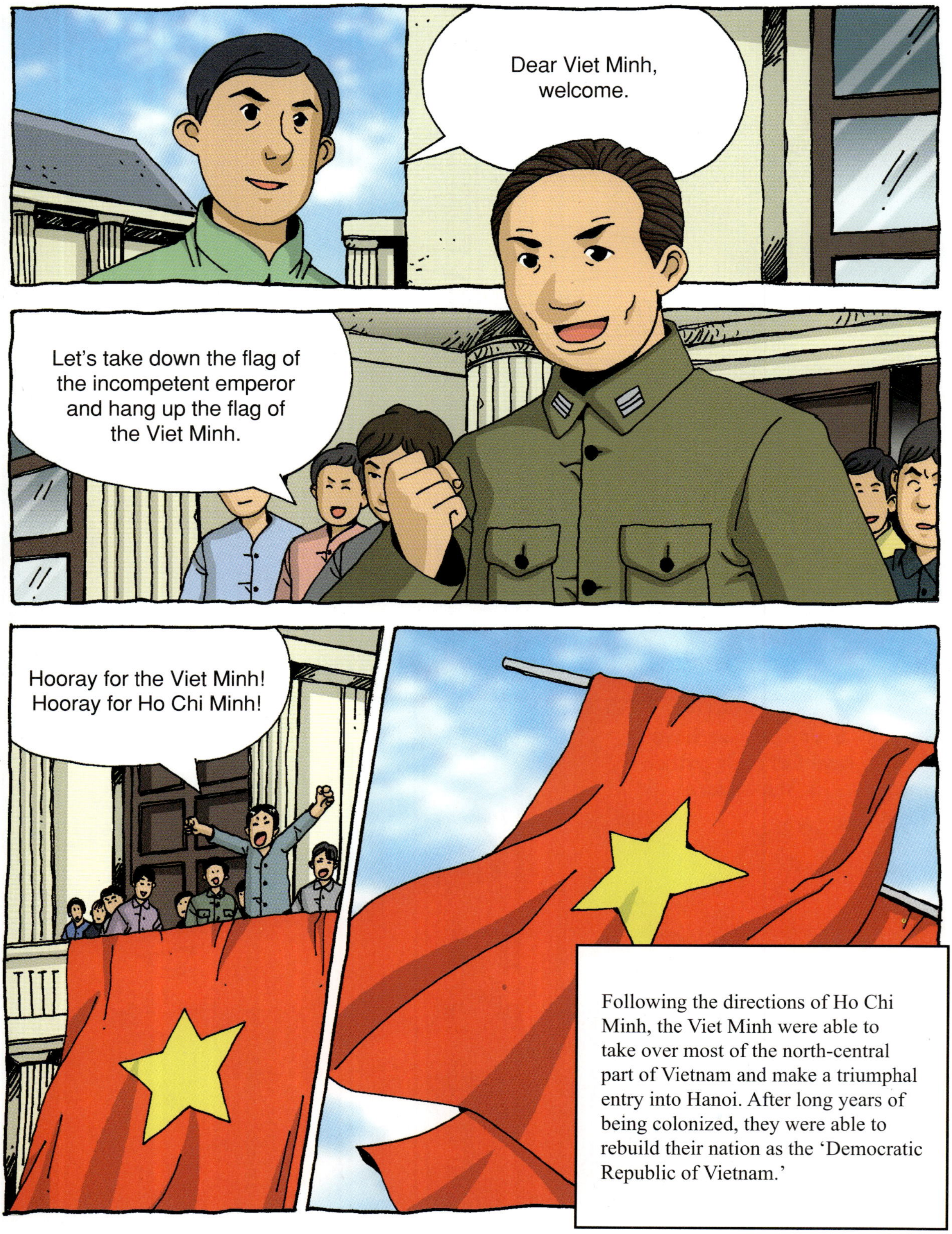

*Premier: The top position in a country or political party, or a person in that position. Similar to prime minister.

The Country that Surprised the World

Thanh did not brag about her brother to others, nor take advantage of his position. She just returned to her hometown and quietly continued with her life.

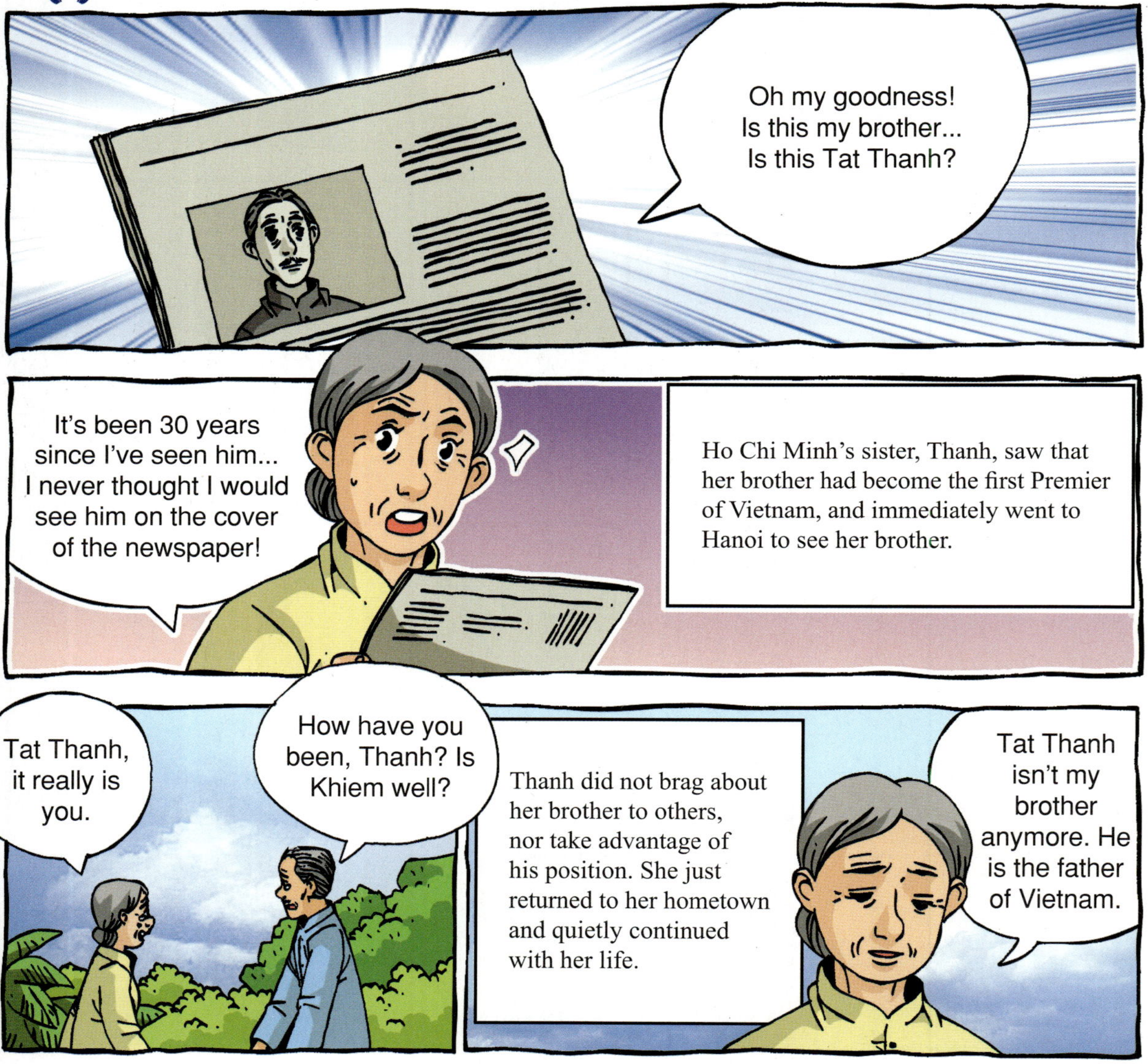

It was the same with his brother. Khiem even stopped people from notifying Ho Chi Minh about his illness since he was afraid of becoming a burden to his famous brother. When Khiem passed away, Ho Chi Minh poured his sorrow into a letter.

I am truly sad. I do not know how to express my sorrow at losing you. But I cannot even be at your funeral, since I am so badly needed to run the country, and your funeral is so very far away. I do not know how I could be forgiven for not looking after my brother. Who should I watch over, if not someone with whom I share blood?

Ho Chi Minh's life did not get any easier even after he became Premier. The Democratic Republic of Vietnam took the northern part of Vietnam where Hanoi was, but the French armies returned to the southern part.

Ho Chi Minh's concerns became reality. In November of 1946, about one year after the Democratic Republic of Vietnam was founded, French armies invaded the north.
BOOM
There is no reason for us to avoid the war if the French want it.
But the French are too strong for us! I insist we take refugee deep in the mountains near Hanoi.
We will be hiding in the mountain jungles during the day, and ambush you at night! While we might only get one of your soldiers for every ten of ours you kill, you will be the ones to leave our country!
Ho Chi Minh and the rest of the Viet Minh leaders escaped to the mountains. Ho Chi Minh left a word of warning to France before leaving Hanoi.
Sir, we are in trouble. The French army came into Hanoi and wiped out our base!
We can't just sit here and watch anymore. We must fight back! Our freedom can be earned through battle.

At 8 p.m. on December 19, 1946, the Viet Minh started a war to fight against the French army. This was the beginning of The First Indochina War. This war was to last for eight years.
Do you see them?
Where'd they go?
Careful, now. If we are caught by the French then it's all over for us. No matter what happens, Mr. Premier, you have to stay alive.
Take out the enemy!
POW POW
BAM
It is as I feared. We are still too weak to fight France.
Everyone, the resistance will be long and it will be painful, but we are not afraid. We need to continue to fight until the day our country, Vietnam, becomes unified and free.

*guerrilla tactics: Attacks made in unexpected places with small numbers of people.

Mr. Premier, please try to rest in between. We don't want you to get sick.
I am fine. Why don't you go ahead and take the night off?
How could we call it a day when you are still up working?
Oh, sorry. I didn't think of that. Let's take a break. Here, drink some water.
Now I see why people refer to him as Uncle Ho.
Hey guys, what if we call this path the Ho Chi Minh Trail? I'd like to think this path will lead us to victory, just like how the Premier is leading the country to victory.

That's a great idea. After all, everyone respects Premier Ho Chi Minh in Vietnam.
Every night, the Viet Minh carried ammunition and food on 'the Ho Chi Minh Trail' through the jungle. The Ho Chi Minh Trail allowed weapons and supplies from the north to be transported around 300 miles through the jungle.

Those clueless French soldiers are probably all fast asleep. They probably think they've won. I doubt they have any idea we are surrounding them.

In 1954, an intense battle took place with the Viet Minh surrounding the French army from high up in the mountain and slowly tightening a circle around the French. Confused, the French soldiers couldn't find a way to escape and surrendered.
H-how could this happen?! We're surrounded by Vietnamese!

Finally, Vietnam had achieved victory at the end of the First Indochina War. But it was decided at a Geneva Convention between international super powers that the country would be divided into North Vietnam and South Vietnam.
They have decided that the Democratic Republic of Vietnam would take the North, and Emperor Bao Dai and his provisional government would rule the South.
This is ridiculous! We can't be insulted like this even after winning a war. Sir, we have to fight again!
That's not an option. Just think about all the suffering that our people have had to go through for the last eight years.
But... but what about...
It might be natural for you to think that we can win again since we have been winning. But the new opponent is America.
The United States had played a large role in dividing Vietnam in half. At the time, the United States was one of the world's two new superpowers, and it was doing brisk business by making and selling weapons for war.

As a country that valued capitalism, the United States was distrustful of all the socialist states that were being created after World War II. To stop this trend, the United States wanted to invade Vietnam to make sure it became a capitalist country.
Once America was our ally, now America has become our greatest threat.
America is emerging as a powerful nation, very different from France, which is finally on the way out. If we act rashly and are not careful, we may not survive.
According to the the Geneva Conventions, there will be an election in two years. Let's wait until then and let the people choose if they want unification.
Yes, Mr. Premier.
During this time, the French army left Vietnam as was decided at the Geneva Convention.
Ho Chi Minh returned to Hanoi without any parades or cheers to welcome him. A victory that saw the country divided in half was not a victory to celebrate.
Mr. Premier, we have prepared a place for you to stay. We renovated the palace where the French governor used to live.

*illiteracy: The inability to read or write.

Thanks to Uncle Ho, women can also learn to read now. We just didn't have the chance until now...

Mr. Premier, do you think I can learn to read, too?

Of course. Just make sure you wear this hat when you are outside as the sun is quite strong.

I'd like to one day be like Uncle Ho. I want to be able to show love to others regardless of their age or class...

Uncle Ho, read to us!

Gather around and take a seat, children. Which story would you like to hear today?

While this was going on in the North, Ngo Dinh Diem took power as dictator over South Vietnam with the support of the United States. He opposed communism and considered Ho Chi Minh to be an enemy that he needed to beat.
No! I was afraid something like this would happen!
A monk burned himself to death to protest Ngo Dinh Diem's corruption, calling him a dictator before he died!
To make matters worse, the president's relatives have taken up all the governor's positions, and his government is terribly corrupt.
Sir, South Vietnam is suppressing Buddhism, but 90% of the Vietnamese there are Buddhist.
This is very troubling. If Ngo Dinh Diem ever lets America get involved, the unification of our country and our people will never happen.
The Americans are coming to Vietnam?

Yes, America will do anything to show off its power. This means we need to strengthen our army as well.
In December of 1960, Ho Chi Minh organized the National Front for the Liberation of South Vietnam, also called the Viet Cong which was able to take over many areas in South Vietnam. After this, as expected, the United States invaded through the Gulf of Tonkin, a port in North Vietnam.
THUD!

The Vietnam War was extremely horrific, and is known as 'the most brutal war in modern history.' The United States poured bombs all over North Vietnam, and soon places across Vietnam were in flames.
The United States is bombing everything in sight, including civilian houses, schools, hospitals, and stores. The United States has dropped 1.5 times more on Vietnam than what was used by all of the Allied forces across the entire world during World War II.
How long can Vietnam stand these attacks from the United States?
Vietnam can last 20, no 100 years. However, I know one thing for sure. We will prevail in the end!

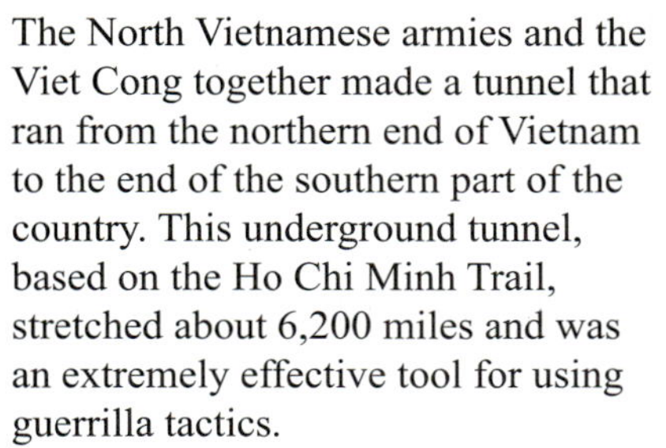

The North Vietnamese armies and the Viet Cong together made a tunnel that ran from the northern end of Vietnam to the end of the southern part of the country. This underground tunnel, based on the Ho Chi Minh Trail, stretched about 6,200 miles and was an extremely effective tool for using guerrilla tactics.

Everyone in Vietnam, including children and females, fought in the war. When the United States' army became restless about being ambushed by not only soldiers, but by villagers, they decided to get rid of the jungle to hinder the guerrilla tactics.

The United States army sprayed a herbicide called Agent Orange over 18% of the Vietnamese land stripping away all the foliage and greenery. In addition, the United States' army continued to commit barbarous acts, such as the mass shootings and killings of many innocent civilians.
You have done well, Mr. Plant, surviving through this. Soon, we'll live in peace.
However, the war united the people and strengthened the resistance even more. When the United States could see that they might lose, they negotiated to withdraw their forces bit by bit.
Finally, the war is coming to an end. Our Premier seems to have found peace as well.

Cough, Cough!
Sir, we have called a doctor for you. Please go inside.
There is no need for that. This is part of nature. I am 80 years old.
You should rest... for a while.
Mr. Premier, your birthday is coming up. Have you considered your birthday wish?
My wish is always the same: Unifying Vietnam on our own.

Ho Chi Minh knew his death was nearing but kept such thoughts to himself and continued to work as if the end of his life was still a long time away.

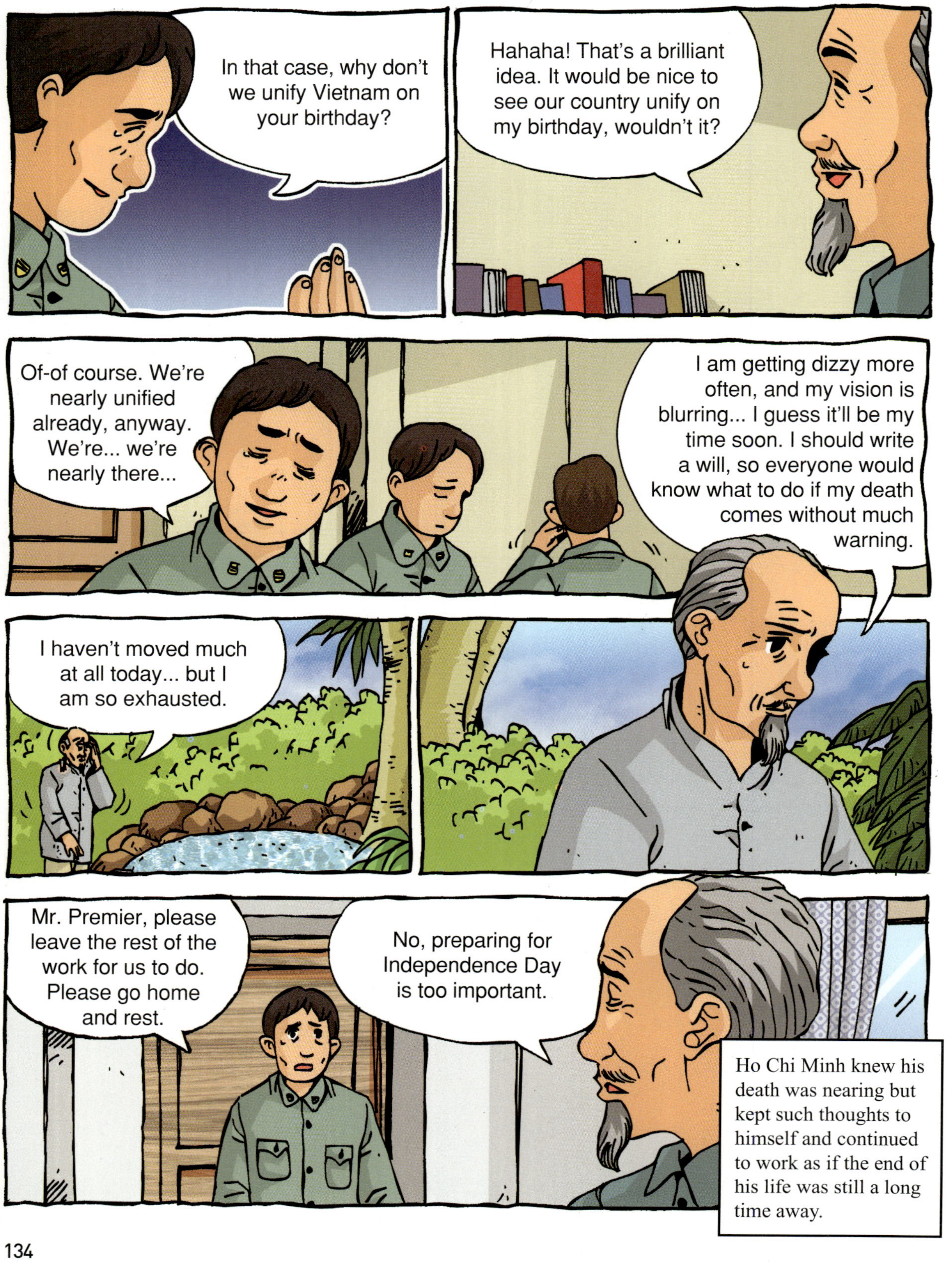

September 2, 1969, on the 24th anniversary of Vietnam's liberation from France, Ho Chi Minh's heart stopped beating forever. All that was left behind of the 79-year-old Ho Chi Minh were a few pieces of worn-out clothing and books. The Vietnamese people felt even greater respect for him when they saw how humbly he had lived.

Tens of thousands of Vietnamese came to Ho Chi Minh's funeral. It was held on a brutally hot summer day, but no one left the place.
Oh, Uncle Ho...

Vietnam stood strong, even after Ho Chi Minh, the leader of the nation, had passed away. Some liked to think it was because every one of them held Uncle Ho in their hearts.
America has been politically unstable recently. This is our chance to drive out the American army from our country.
Absolutely. Let's call this last strategy to unify our country the 'Ho Chi Minh Campaign.'

Yes. The Ho Chi Minh Campaign will lead our country to unification. It is what he always wanted.
In March of 1975, Vietnam's last offensive against the United States and the South Vietnamese government, the Ho Chi Minh Campaign, was launched.

Proceed!
Do it for a united Vietnam!

We have huge obstacles to overcome, but Vietnam will remain strong! For victory, everyone fight with all you've got!
We want unification! Americans, go home!

Oh no, the North Vietnamese are closing in on our position, retreat!

All American military forces, sound the retreat!

RUMBLE RUMBLE
This is strange. Why is it so quiet?
Did the American army already leave?
If they're gone, then we should go to the American embassy!

The U.S. army has already retreated. The last of them left in a helicopter from the American embassy.
Cowards! We scared them off!

Hahaha! Finally the North and South have become one nation! Hooray for the Democratic Republic of Vietnam! Hooray for the Ho Chi Minh Campaign!

On April 30, 1975, once North Vietnamese soldiers confirmed that the U.S. army had left, they lowered the flag of South Vietnam and raised the flag of the Democratic Republic of Vietnam. The Vietnam War, which had lasted ten years, was the first war that the world's most powerful and wealthiest country, the United States, had lost.

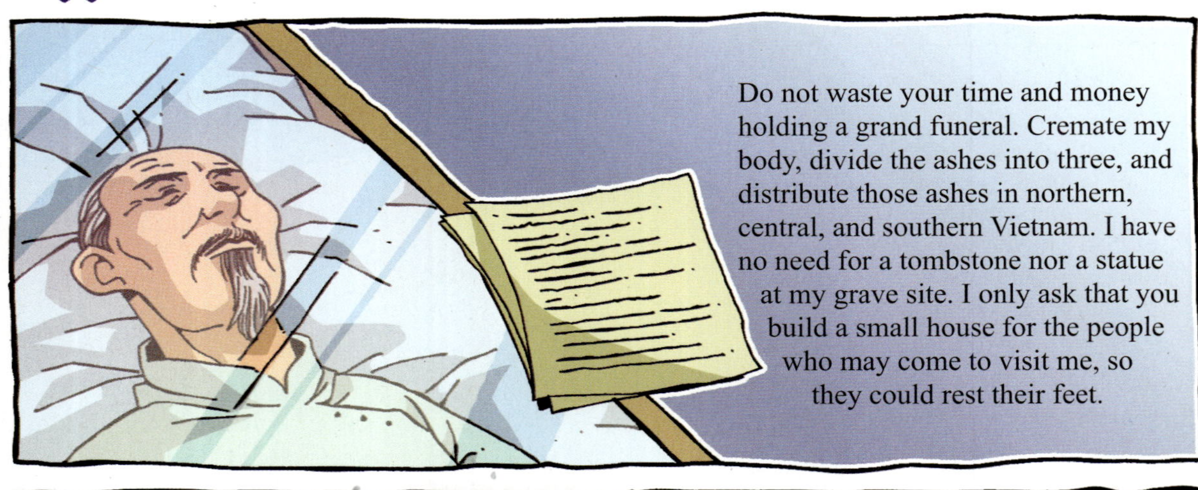

Ho Chi Minh did not want to waste people's taxes on his funeral. But in the end, his body was embalmed and placed in Ba Dinh Square in Hanoi, the capital city of the newly unified Vietnam.

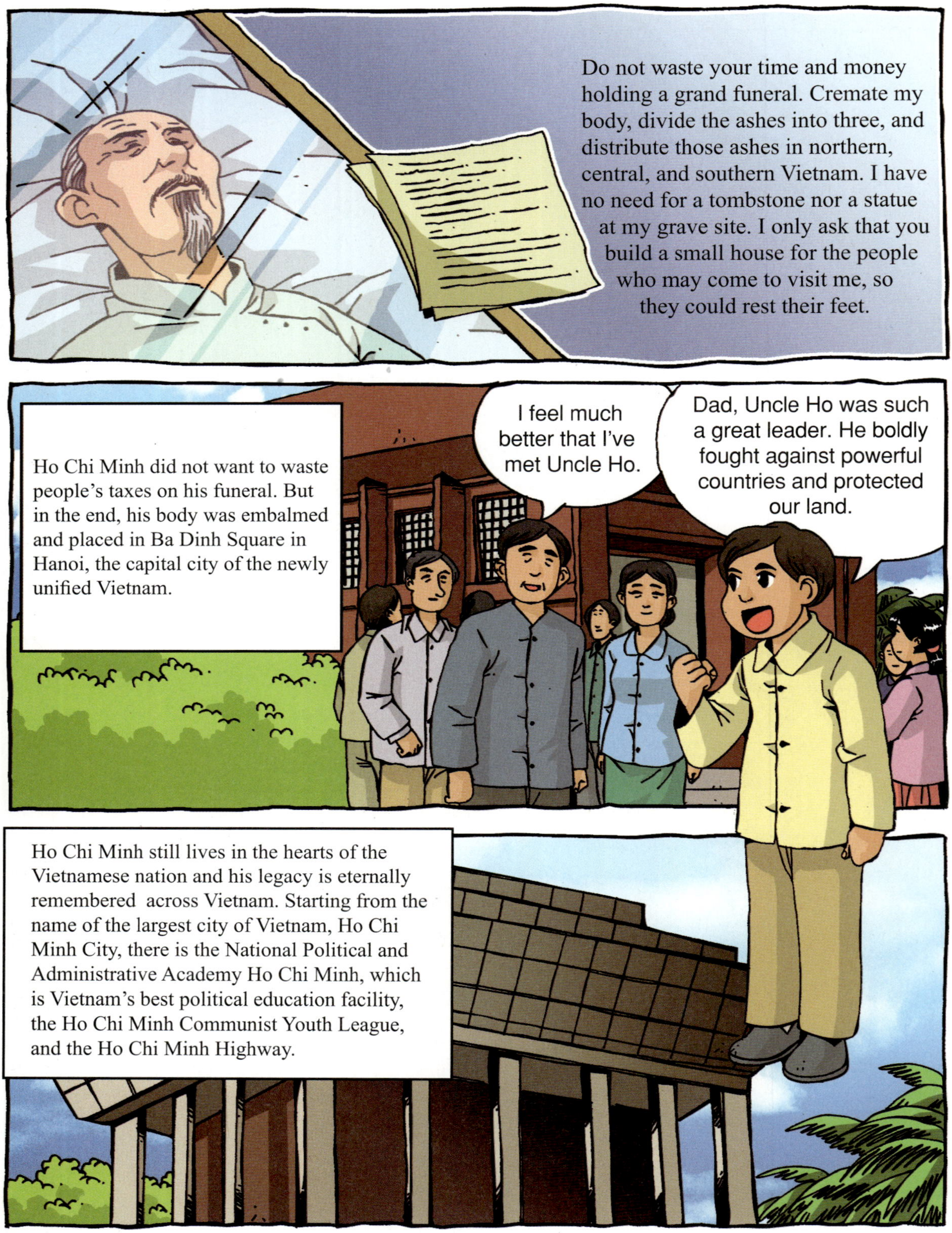

Ho Chi Minh still lives in the hearts of the Vietnamese nation and his legacy is eternally remembered across Vietnam. Starting from the name of the largest city of Vietnam, Ho Chi Minh City, there is the National Political and Administrative Academy Ho Chi Minh, which is Vietnam's best political education facility, the Ho Chi Minh Communist Youth League, and the Ho Chi Minh Highway.

The day Ho Chi Minh's passing was announced, countries all over the world sent their condolences and paid tribute to his accomplishments and honored his character. Even the United States, contributed praise of the man. As recorded in the newspaper *The New York Times*' obituary, "the small, frail, ivory like figure of Ho... was that of a patriarch, the George Washington of his nation."
TIME magazine put Ho Chi Minh's face on the cover and said of him that "no national leader alive today has stood so stubbornly for so long before the enemy's guns."
A man with a heart as big as the heavens, a man who had endless love for children, a man with supreme earthly power but who refused to live in comfort or enjoy wealth and honor: this man was Ho Chi Minh. Today, the Vietnamese still remember and honor the leader who always put the happiness of his people before his own life.

Word Search

● Find the words which are hidden horizontally, vertically and diagonally.

```
S M Z G Q M Z G Q M Z G Q J M Z G Q M X
G R I E F E N T I O N H W I N A H C N O
E B N J A B Q J E T E A R B A R I O B M
R V D P R D C K R V V K G R V E K M V F
E C E O A S E N T C A L T T C S U K C E
V X P Q Y N D O Y X N Q Y Y Y P N O X M
E Z E W U D I E C Z M W R U Z E J N Z W
A N N E I A E O S A E Z E I A C A E A I
L S D R O S G C N E L R H O S T S R S T
G D E U P D H T O D R E O P D H T B U P
A F N Y H F U Y A T C V H A F U Y I F L
S G C U S T I N C R A G E I N G U T F A
T H E I D H M I D H L I R D H O I Y E U
O J A B S O R A F J T J A F J T J F R S
R K I N D L E O R T I O N A T E B G K X
H L A N H L E N H E E N H H L E N H L B
J Q T M J Q T A U T D O R I T Y M J B L
S P A R K L I N G W Y Q L N W Y Q L U E
Z A R E H E N T Z B K F Z M S U F T J R
X E M J X M R I N C P O B R A V E X N M
W R Q F C R Q C P R O P H X R Q C V R P
```

| independence | sparkling | deserve | grief |
| kindle | suffer | respect | brave |

Vocabulary

● Match each word to the correct meaning.

1. liberty	• 도둑
2. colony	• 해결책
3. twinkle	• 자유
4. resistance	• 달아나다
5. attack	• 요구
6. thief	• 공격하다
7. run away	• 식민지
8. class	• 저항
9. valuable	• 계급
10. Confucianism	• 가치 있는
11. demand	• 반짝거리다
12. solution	• 유교

Guess What?

● Guess what he said in the blank.

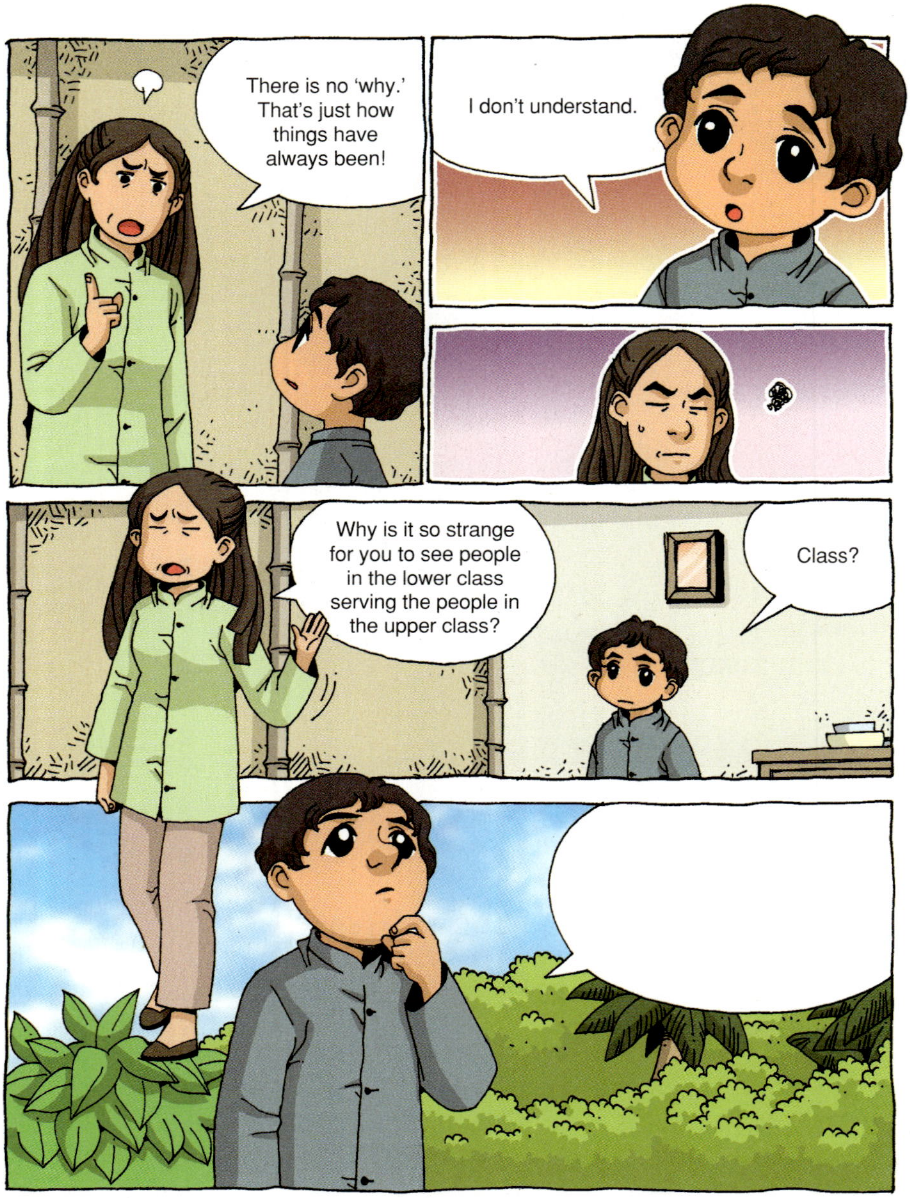

Lesson 4

Southeast Asia

In southeast Asia, there are some hot and humid countries such as Vietnam, Cambodia, and Thailand. And each country has a unique history and culture. Can you name the countries and find them on the map?

<Southeast Asia Map>

Quizzes

● Write down the country's name in each blank.

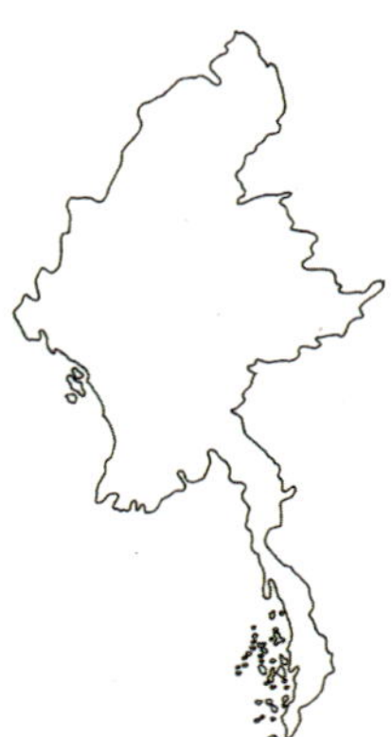

1. ______________________________

This country was called Burma before. The capital city is Rangoon. There are mysterious beautiful ancient golden pagodas in the city.

2. ______________________________

This country is the largest and most varied archipelago on Earth, with over 18,000 counted islands including Sumatra and Java. Its Bali is world famous as a resort island.

3. ______________________________

This country is surrounded by the Pacific Ocean, consisting of 7,107 islands. The capital city is Manila. They speak in Filipino and English in the country.

4. ______________________________

This country experiences tropical weather all year round. The capital city is Kuala Lumpur where towering skyscrapers look down upon wooden houses built on stilts.

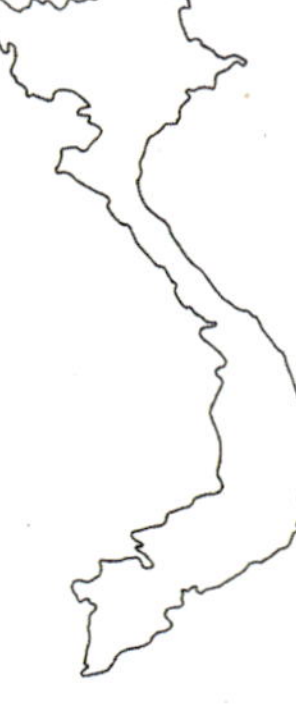

5. ______________________________

The capital city of this country is Hanoi. Ho Chi Minh was Prime Minister and President of this country. The beautiful UNESCO site, Halong Bay is located in the northwest of this country.

6. ______________________

The capital city is Phnom Penh. Mekong River
crosses the entire country. This country is famous
for the mysterious ancient temple of Angkor Wat.

7. ______________________

The capital city is Bangkok. This country is famous for its beautiful
beaches including Phuket Island. 95 % of the people is Buddhist.

8. ______________________

People speak Mandarin, English, Malay, Hokkien,
and Cantonese in the country. Although it is a small
country located on the southern edge of Malaysia,
the country is modern international seaport city.

9. ______________________

This country is bordered by Thailand, China, Myanmar,
Vietnam, and Cambodia. The official language is Lao.

10. ______________________

The country is on the northwestern edge of Borneo Island.
The king of this country is one of the richest man in the
world. There is no taxes in this country.

Answers: 1. Myanmar   2. Indonesia   3. Philippines   4. Malaysia   5. Vietnam

6. Cambodia   7. Thailand   8. Singapore   9. Laos   10. Brunei

1890년		5월 19일, 베트남의 작은 농촌 마을인 킴리엔에서 태어났습니다.
1908년	18세	농민들의 세금 반대 시위에 참여했다는 이유로 국립 학교인 '꾸옥혹'에서 퇴학당합니다.
1911년	21세	프랑스 배의 보조 요리사로 취직을 한 후, 배를 타고 세계 여러 나라를 돌아다닙니다.
1919년	29세	'응우옌 아이 꾸옥'이란 이름으로 〈베트남 민족의 요구〉라는 글을 발표합니다.
1923년	33세	계속되는 프랑스 경찰의 감시를 피해 모스크바로 탈출하여 군대를 기르는 법, 사람들을 끌어 모으는 법 등 혁명에 필요한 교육을 받습니다.
1925년	35세	중국 광저우에서 베트남 학생들을 가르치며, '베트남 혁명 청년회'를 만들고 「청년」지를 창간합니다.
1930년	40세	'베트남공산당'을 창당합니다.
1931년	41세	6월, 홍콩에서 영국경찰에 체포되어 감옥에 갇혔다가 다음 해 12월에 석방됩니다.
1940년	50세	'베트남 독립 동맹(베트민)'을 출범시킵니다. 이때부터 호치민이라는 이름을 사용하기 시작합니다.
1941년	51세	비밀리에 베트남에 입국하여 팍 보 마을의 동굴에서 생활하며 「독립 베트남」을 창간합니다.
1944년	54세	'베트남 해방군'부대를 만듭니다.

1945년	55세	제2차 세계 대전이 끝나고 일본이 항복하자 '베트남 민주 공화국' 임시 정부를 수립하고 초대 주석이 됩니다.
1946년	56세	프랑스와 협상에 실패하여 하노이에서 제1차 인도차이나 전쟁이 시작됩니다.
1948년	58세	3월, 남베트남에서 프랑스의 지원 아래 전 황제 바오다이가 임시정부를 수립합니다.
1954년	64세	디엔비엔푸 전투에서 크게 승리하고 프랑스군을 몰아내지만, 이번엔 프랑스 대신 미국이 남베트남에 들어옵니다.
1959년	69세	12월, '남베트남 민족 해방 전선'을 수립합니다.
1964년	74세	8월, 미군이 통킹 만을 폭격하고 제2차 인도차이나 전쟁(베트남 전쟁)이 벌어집니다.
1969년	79세	9월 2일, 베트남이 통일되는 순간을 보지 못하고 세상을 떠납니다.
1973년		미국이 휴전을 선언하고, 미군 부대 전면 철수를 합의합니다.
1975년		4월 30일, 베트남 인민군이 마지막 공세를 펴, 사이공을 점령합니다.
1976년		남베트남과 북베트남이 통일되어 '통일 베트남 사회주의 공화국'이 수립됩니다.

Note